ON WRITING

ON WRITING

by *ROGER SALE*

University of Washington

RANDOM HOUSE

New York

For
The Bounders

CONTENTS

[vii]

ON WRITING

INTRODUCTION

This book is not, strictly speaking, about how to write English. It is not a handbook about topic sentences or the comma splice, and it is not a rhetoric about the various levels of tone and diction. Nor is it about the teaching of English, though it is the result of the efforts of one English teacher's having tried to teach some students who were trying to learn. It is a book about a particular kind of writing written all over America today: the English paper.

In an ideal world the English paper would not be a separate genre, but that ours is not an ideal world can best be indicated here with a story. Not long ago I had a conversation with a freshman at the University of Washington whom I had known for a number of years, but not as a student. She had never done strikingly well in school, and she was not at the moment doing strikingly well in her English course. Yet I had received a number of personal letters from her that were lucid, relaxed, a pleasure to read.

So I asked her, "Julie, why don't you write your English papers the way you write letters? They are clear as can be, and I know you don't spend lots of time fussing over them."

Her reply was quick and decisive: "But I can't write *that* way. Not on an *English* paper."

The difference between Julie and most students is simply that she is more honest: she had let the cat out of the bag. English

[3]

papers are formal, impersonal, organized, careful about matters of technique, and, one need hardly add, quite quite dead. Letters, on the other hand, are relaxed, personal, occasionally sloppy, and more like speech than like English papers. Book reports, themes, debates, and term papers fall into one category, while letters, diaries, journals, and conversations fall into another. English papers are written for teachers, for classrooms, for adults, to fulfill assignments; letters or diaries are written for oneself or one's contemporaries. The division is clear in the minds of good students, less clear but equally real in the minds of bad students.

There is perhaps no better way to indicate the bias of this book than to speak briefly about what I mean by "good students" and "bad students" and what I take to be their similarities and differences. A "good student" is one who has learned how to "do" school, who sees what is asked of him by his teachers, and who knows how to go about performing in ways acceptable to them. He has a sound, instinctive grasp of English grammar, he knows how to make an outline, how to do research problems, how to compile a bibliography, how to write topic sentences and concluding paragraphs. Often he does not know that he knows how to do these things, but he has sat in English or Language Arts classes ever since he can remember, and somehow he does what they require competently. In the fourth grade he can answer questions like, "What is the climax of this story?"; in the sixth grade he can write capsule biographies of Abraham Lincoln or John F. Kennedy; in the eighth grade he can write a short story from his personal experience which makes his life sound exciting or funny; in high school he writes themes on the themes of the Book of Job and research papers on the background of the present crisis in the Middle East; in college he analyzes poems so as to show he can recognize and describe their structure and their symbols. The "good student," thus, is extremely adaptable. He has been going to school all his life, he has taken courses from as many as thirty English teachers, for each one of whom he discovers a way of writing that seems called for at the moment.

The "good student" probably has recognized now and again in his long career as a writer that what he does is somehow unreal or phony. Often he can tell because of the way he shoves the rest of his life out of the way when he has "an English paper due tomorrow." Faced with this task, he sits down, maybe makes an outline, looks over his class notes or goes back through the passages he has underlined in the text. If he is very fluent he can soon sense how to begin, what kind of introductory paragraph to write. He may be able to turn out a 500-word essay for a freshman English course in an hour, and he can figure, as he finishes, that once again he has gotten the world off his back. Perhaps at that moment he can recognize in himself a conscious shifting of mental gears as he drops the self that writes English papers and reestablishes the other selves presently available. It is as though he becomes a different person when he writes his English papers, and their tone is almost always a tone more knowing and wise than he uses anywhere else. If told there is something phony about this business of writing English papers, he might object; yet, as he sets the world aside to write and brings it back when he is finished, he is in effect saying, "This is special labor, and in order to do it I cannot be at all the same me that talks to a friend or has parents or likes to drive cars at very high speeds."

The "bad student" is different only because he does what the "good student" does but does it more slowly and less well. He is trying to be like the "good student"; he wants to be fluent and to make the writing of an English paper into a perfectible, special talent. But he probably does not see easily where to begin a paper, he starts sentences he does not know how to finish and lurches this way and that without ever seeing any good way to control his paper. He takes up to four hours to do less well what the "good student" does in forty-five minutes. He daydreams, gets up and combs his hair, calls a friend or gets a coke, and with each interruption his chances for a smooth and neatly worked out paper diminish, because it becomes harder and harder for him to remember what he was writing about, where he thought it might go, how it might look when he finished. But though he takes longer and gets a C or D instead of a B or an A, the "bad student" is working on the same track as the "good student." The two are not qualitatively different from each other. Both know what an English paper is and how it differs from every other kind of writing or speaking either has encountered. The difference is simply that the "bad student" does not know how to do it and the "good student" does.

Below are the beginnings of two paragraphs, one written by the "good student," the other by the "bad student." It takes little discernment to tell who wrote which. Both are writing on the topic: "If you want to know what God thinks of money, look at the people He gives it to."

> I'm not sure how to respond to people who have money, but I can talk about those who don't. A family may be poor and wonder how bills can be paid, but they can be rich in all that really counts in life—in love and family strength.

> In our country the rich are very rich. If you look around, the average person isn't rich and maybe he doesn't even want to be. Whether a man is rich depends mostly on how hard he wants to work to be rich.

Neither of these beginnings is very promising, but instinctively most readers will say the first is better than the second. Yet it is much easier to say what is wrong with the second than it is to say what is right with the first. Faced with the second, all teachers and most students can open up their bags of phrases: the connection between the three sentences is unclear; the second half of the second sentence has little to do with the first half; the "you" of the if-clause disappears without explanation; the word "rich" is used, unnecessarily, five times in three sentences. In neither form nor content is there any consecutiveness or sense of direction.

In contrast, the first beginning is neat and direct: poor people can be rich too. Furthermore, all the obvious objections to the second beginning imply that it ought to be more like the first. It wavers, stutters, slides, and the first does not. A busy teacher could comment on the second paper as I have done above and soon have a comment even longer than the writer's original sentences. The comment would say all the things the writer of the second beginning has been told ever since he began taking English courses: if you want a paper with fewer red marks on it, if you want a better grade, clean up your writing, tighten it, neaten it, control it—make it "good writing."

Most books on writing, especially the less theoretical ones, concern themselves implicitly with the writer of the second beginning, the "bad student." They try to show someone how to overcome the slipping and the stuttering and the general air of incoherence that is characteristic of inferior writing. This book does not shun such a writer for its audience, but its message to him is no different than its message to the writer of the first beginning, the "good student": there are better things to be as a writer than a "good student." (At this point I will drop the quotation marks around "good student" and "bad student" and hope my reasons for using them in the first place are clear. These terms will continue to mean what they mean here throughout the book. The phrase "good writer," though, is intended to mean someone who at least *seeks* to write well.) For it seems to me that the proper response to both beginnings is a defeated sigh. To tell the writer of the second merely what is wrong with what he has done is only to encourage him to try to be more like the writer of the first, as though one of the necessary stages in his development as a writer is his transformation into a good student. In fact, it is often as easy to help a bad student become a good writer as it is to help a good student become a good writer, because the good student tends to resist the idea that there is something wrong with what he does and feels he is being asked to exchange his fluency as a writer for some will-o'-the-wisp he barely understands and which no one can easily define for him. The bad student, figuring he has little to lose, is more willing to take chances.

The great difficulty facing the good student is that all too often he is ignored. The two sentences of his writing quoted above are not illiterate, but they are dead, unthinking, uncaring, uncivilized. This is a serious charge and one that would take the best of teachers a long time to demonstrate properly. Most teachers do not have this kind of time, and many are not interested in devoting their time to showing what is wrong with the writing of a good student. On the flyleaf of many books about writing are lists of symbols many teachers put in the margins of the papers of bad students; but there are no symbols to explain to the good student what is wrong. He has made his truce with English teachers and English papers, and most teachers and most assignments will honor that truce and make no comment. Depending on how advanced a course and how severe a teacher he has, he will receive a grade ranging from C minus all the way up to A minus, but in all likelihood the grade will come without comment, and so the good student will have gotten by once again.

"A family may be poor and wonder how bills can be paid, but they can be rich in all that really counts in life." The writer is not really trying, and he does not want his teacher to try either. If I read that and were in a not very good mood I might write in the margin something like "Scout's honor?" If I were in a pleasant mood I would probably write, "*All* that counts?" In either event the writer will feel insulted, but he will probably not see that he has implicitly insulted me with his plump recitation of the homely virtues. Is this writer trying to tell me anything I have not heard many many times, in magazines, over loudspeakers, and set to music? Or that he has not heard almost as often as I? This student is not a writer, only a copyist of the words of others, and of others who also were not trying to say anything. Does he think I have never been told that the love of money is the root of all evil? Does he think I have never heard "Home, Sweet Home"? Does he think I was never told the story of King Midas? Who does he think I am? Obviously he thinks or hopes I will not care who I am or who he is and will for the moment be satisfied with the grammatical correctness of his prose.

What makes all this difficult to say is that the good student, even when he writes as unthinkingly as he has in this case, is only doing as he has been taught to do and doing what he has found sufficient to get him out of a situation not of his own choosing and not much to his liking. He may in many other respects be alive, thoughtful, caring, and civilized; he may be able to solve sophisticated problems in mathematics or chemistry; he may be able to handle himself in social situations that require sensitivity and subtlety. But as a writer, he is rude, a barbarian. The more he is admirable in other ways, the more he deserves to be told this, and in ways he can understand and not be insulted by.

Most teachers and a great many students sense or know that the writing of English papers has many aspects of being a waste of time; certainly there are few people who would proclaim with any fervor that writing is taught and learned in this country as well as it might be. Mass literacy inevitably produces mass semiliteracy, many people who cannot easily or naturally use the written word in order to tell someone they do not know intimately what is on their minds. This is not a situation simply to be deplored, especially when one imagines the alternatives. But it is nothing to be terribly happy about either. Broad cultural analyses we have aplenty, but teachers of composition have not often addressed themselves in writing to the task they implicitly address all the time in the classroom: how to tell someone the difference between good English and good writing. We have books galore on the difference between good English and bad English, and an even larger number that seem to assume that learning to write is only an adjunct or a side effect of learning to read literature. But we do not have many books which speak to those teachers and students mentioned above who feel that good writing is a matter of great importance which seems to get lost in the welter of assignments, papers, and corrections that all too often is the essence of courses in English or Language Arts.

This book tries to deal with writing as it is presently taught and learned in classrooms in America. I like to think of the book as being practical, sensible, helpful, idealistic, hopeful, as developing arguments and distinctions which may, indeed, tell some students things they had never thought about before. It is, for reasons I hope I have made clear already and will keep on making clear on every page, not a book that tells anyone how to write; I don't think that can be done. It tries to talk about writing and the conditions under which writing is done in ways that will encourage people to ask more of themselves.

It has not been easy for me to gauge exactly what I seek or hope my audience to be. Nor is this easy for me to describe now. I would like to say that any member of that group engaged in the teaching and learning of writing, mostly in the formal circumstances of courses and classrooms, is my audience. But almost certainly that is too ambitious a statement. Language Arts is taught in the seventh grade, and scholarly writing is taught by directors of Ph.D. dissertations; I would be both immodest and unwise to claim teachers and students in these groups as part of my audience. On the other hand, most books of this kind are directed solely at students in freshman English courses —not at high school seniors, not at college sophomores, not even at teachers of the freshmen—and that seems to me an audience so narrowly conceived as to abuse and distort the tone of books addressed to such a group. I think of my potential readers as teachers and students in high school and college. Most of what I say is directed at students, to be sure, but it should become clear in Chapter 2 that I think the problem is one that involves all of us. I include a number of papers in the chapters that follow, but the problems they raise are not just problems for students. How does one respond to these papers? What questions does one ask about them? How would one want them different? These are teachers' questions, but not exclusively; anyone can be concerned—with the writing, the response, the questions.

I shall now describe, in a general way, what happens in succeeding chapters. The general proposition of Chapter 2 is that writing can be learned, but it can't be taught. I do not know who first formulated this phrase. Probably it was first said in just that way fairly recently, though earlier writers would have immediately assented to the proposition and wondered about the good sense of people who thought otherwise. We often forget that the idea of teaching writing as we know it is a recent idea and a distinctly American one. Chapter 2, then, is about courses in writing, about the assumptions students and teachers make concerning each other that often are almost disastrous for good writing or even for good relations between the two groups. My experience is, of course, limited by the simple fact that the classes I know most about were taught by me, and I have been forced to learn about how others teach and learn at secondhand. Often, therefore, I say that this or that happens in classrooms without being able to know, in fact, how many teachers or students I am talking about. I have seen many assignments other teachers have handed out, have listened to many teachers and students talk about what goes on in their classrooms, but, at best, my experience in this line is woefully limited. Still, within this limited range, it is experience I believe to be representative. The two schools at which I have taught, for instance, are in many ways very much unlike each other, yet the students I have taught and the testimony they have offered lead me to believe that in this country most teaching of writing follows certain familiar patterns. I have tried to describe these patterns, to criticize the activities that comprise them, and to offer some alternative ways of thinking of teaching and learning that might liberate writing from the bondage it is often forced to suffer.

The rest of the book considers matters more usually thought of as within the province of textbooks on writing. In Chapter 3 I take up in some detail various matters that come under the heading of "Organization." The aim is to argue against learning outlining and other means of organizing which lead people to think that someone else can tell them how their papers should be organized before they write them. Most of the time, it seems to me, students are encouraged to think of the larger matters of organization in ways that discourage them from asking themselves, sentence-by-sentence as they write, how *this* is related to *that*, how *that* fits into the *other thing*. I first take up a cluster of small but crucial matters of organization at the level of word, phrase, and sentence; I then consider the consequences of this way of thinking about small matters for the way a paper is organized paragraph-by-paragraph; finally, I discuss the combination of "small" and "large" matters to create a single forward motion.

In Chapter 4, which is about a host of problems that usually come under the headings of "Style" and "Grammar," I try to make sense out of various questions that are often asked but seldom answered well: what is a cliche and what is wrong with one? what is jargon and what is wrong with it? what are dangling modifiers and comma splices and tense shifts? what is the difference between "uninterested" and "disinterested"? what are the reasons for resisting some developments in the language and welcoming some others? I do not pretend to do more than give examples of things and try to show how sense can be made of some matters about which most students feel arbitrary decisions and customs always prevail. As a result, this chapter cannot, practically speaking, serve as a handbook of all questions of style and usage, though it does concern itself with matters covered by such handbooks.

I have been mindful, in writing this book, that the study of writing often involves the study of language—linguistics or semantics—and also that both grammar and rhetoric are classical disciplines. But often discussion of these matters carries with it an air of unreality. Let me offer a familiar example. One of the major concerns of rhetoric is the matter of audience, and most textbooks spend a lot of time talking about the way a writer defines or reaches his audience. It is obvious that writing intended for the intimate perusal of a friend is not going to be the same as writing intended for a large audience of strangers. But it is even more obvious that writing done by students is written for the audience of the single person who is the writer's teacher. The teacher is not an intimate friend of the student; neither is he a total stranger. This is not to say that a teacher is not an audience, of course, but in textbooks like this one there is little point to discussions of how to gain and keep the attention of a mass audience of strangers. The teacher knows what assignments he made, has read whatever reading he has assigned, but has no way of knowing what a student thinks until the student makes those thoughts intelligible in language.

Another problem that has come down to us from the tradition of rhetoric involves the use of the first person singular. For reasons I have never quite understood, many teachers tell their students never to use "I" in their papers. Perhaps already a great many readers of these pages have wondered if it is really all right for me to be so free with "I" and "me," and have wanted me, in effect, to use certain other phrases, most of which imply that I didn't do the writing. Some kinds of writing, of course, cannot use the first person singular because the writer is speaking for a group: laws, legal briefs, committee reports, national proclamations, newspaper editorials. In any kind of writing, furthermore, it *may* serve a writer's purpose not to use "I" and "me." But in any writing done by an individual who is speaking in his own voice, "I" or "me" or "it seems to me," and the like are all potentially useful words and phrases. Often it is helpful to say "I think" in order to indicate that what the writer thinks is not the prevailing opinion of the majority. Often "I" is called for because in fact "I" is meant: "I conclude from this" is almost always preferable to some clumsy phrase like "It can be concluded . . ." or "The conclusion one can draw . . ." So, too, "one" has very real uses when the intent is to create the equivalent of what in legal terms is called the "reasonable man." "One does not want jargon cluttering up his sentences" does not simply mean that I have this eccentric bias against jargon; it means that as far as I can see no one wants to clutter his sentences with jargon.

But in all these matters common sense is possible, and perhaps all I mean when I say that my aim in this book is straightforward and practical is that I am trying to be sensible about the writing done in English courses. This in itself betrays a kind of bias, and along the way I will probably say things that someone else could look at and say, "He's following so-and-so's method," or "His assumptions about linguistics and reality are positivistic." Anything can be made to serve abstract aims and goals, but I have not here had any such aims or goals in mind. English courses are not going to be abolished in the near future; how, then, can courses in writing and the writing done in them be thought and talked about so as to make sense? I offer no system and can make no promise that someone who reads this book will become a better writer. What I hope is that someone will feel, after he has finished, that this one small part of life can be more interesting, more sensibly and clearly thought about, and more able to engage and challenge his most intelligent energy than he once found it to be.

2

WRITING CAN BE LEARNED BUT IT CAN'T BE TAUGHT

*Writing Considered as a
Mechanical Skill*

When we speak of something as a mechanical process, we usually mean that its performance involves a series of set, repeatable steps, and often we mean that these steps can be listed or diagrammed in ways easy for others to understand. Repairing an automobile is a mechanical skill, as is operating a lathe and swimming the butterfly stroke. Anyone who does these activities well has developed his instincts to the point that often his hands and eyes and arms can do the job without great conscious effort on his part. First this, then that, then the other thing and, given practice, these "steps" can be reduced to simple fluid motion. Anyone who has tried to teach someone else a skill that has become habitual for himself suddenly remembers how many small steps are involved. Down on the clutch, shift into first, down on the gas, up on the clutch, then shift into second. It *is* a process, its steps can be described easily, and we all know that the process will not work if we try to omit or transpose one or more steps.

Some mechanical skills are, of course, much harder than others. It is easier to ride a bicycle than to drive a car; it is easier to drive a car than to repair one. But it is fun to be expert at performing even fairly simple operations like driving a nail or wiring an outlet or changing a tire. Our pleasure when we first learn to do something like this can easily survive the scorn of the bystander who says, "That's easy." Starting a fire, chopping a log, serving a tennis ball—these are all skills in which

[15]

it is possible to become truly expert, but in which it is possible for someone merely competent to feel some pride. When we first learn, we can say, "Now I've got it, first this and then that," and at some point later on when we have gotten pretty good we can say, "This is not just a skill; there's an art to doing this just right."

Our usual thinking about mechanical skills makes two related distinctions. First we distinguish between the expert and the bungler within almost every skill, and second we distinguish between skills that are harder to learn or to master than others. In both, a sense of art or special talent comes into play. We may say as we watch a taxi driver maneuver through jammed streets, "There is an artist at work," but that is a special use of the word "artist." What we really mean is that driving a car is fairly easy to do and that the taxi driver can do that fairly easy thing very well, better than we can. But we all feel that if we aren't terribly clumsy we could learn to be as good as the taxi driver. We admire his expertise just as we deplore and are frightened of bad, careless drivers, though what is involved isn't really beyond the skill of the average man.

Other skills, however, are more difficult, so much so that we even resist the idea of thinking of them as set, repeatable processes at all. One can find directions for playing the French horn, but anyone who has picked up a horn and followed the directions knows that only gurgles and snorts come out. One dentist may say to another dentist, "All you do is this, and then that, and the rest is easy," but we know better than to try ourselves. A teacher or a lawyer may and often must establish certain routines, but we all know that teachers and lawyers who really do operate routinely are not very good. "Just keep them stirred up" or "Say it like it is" may seem like reasonable mottoes to offer beginning teachers, but no one can say how you do these things. The great ballet dancer Nijinsky thought what he did with extraordinary grace and ease could be reduced to a process: "I just leap up and then stay there."

There is, to be sure, writing, and then there is writing. "He's a *writer*" or "He's got *talent*" implies the man does not simply write, but either that he writes very well or else is famous or lives on what he writes. Whatever is involved here, it is usually assumed to be quite different from the writing taught in schools. Writers are grouped with painters, composers, conductors, ballet dancers, perhaps with show business people, perhaps with The Arts; for better or worse, depending on one's preferences or prejudices, these are a group apart. What is involved in being A Writer is "talent" or "genius" and living in garrets or having brainstorms or maybe just having "a way" with words. But such writing is considered special because it cannot be taught as a skill by English teachers; indeed, one myth has it that English teachers are the enemies of "true" or "real" artists. If we are going to consider writing as a mechanical skill we seem, at least so the myths argue, forced to forget literature, talent, imagination, and the like, and to talk about grammar, drills, themes, or papers—the writing that gets us moved from one English course to the next in schools.

Writing as Taught in Most Schools and Colleges

By the time anyone learns to write he has already learned how to speak in rather complex ways, and in most schools it is presumed that writing must be taught almost as something totally distinct from speaking. The first writing is usually copying, and in early stages writing skill is the same as handwriting skill. This is taught, and learned with varying degrees of success, almost entirely as mechanical action: to make a *b* the semicircle goes to the right of the line, to make a *d* it goes to the left, and so on. Then spelling comes into play, and most of it is taught mechanically; this is followed by some rudimentary grammar. Children learn to write an "e" and then to spell "there," and then to tell "there" from "their." At a certain stage "Handwriting" or the equivalent ceases to be a subject and so no longer appears on report cards; some time later "Spelling" ceases to be a subject, and only "English," or "Language Arts," as it is now called, remains. About this time "teacher" is replaced by "English teacher," and that implies the subject is now complicated enough to require a specialist.

This whole enterprise is a set, repeatable process and almost every one of the small steps along the way is taught and learned as a set, repeatable process. We know this is so because anyone who fails to learn one of the operations is not allowed to continue on to the next one, as though doing handwriting before spelling were like putting the car in gear before releasing the clutch. Students have been kept in the second grade an extra year because their teacher could not decipher their printing. At later stages students will be kept from "advanced" or the next year's "Language Arts" class because they cannot spell, write complete sentences, or learn standard procedures for something known as "paragraphing." Some of these students will be put into remedial sections, now never called remedial but "basic" or "improvement" or even "enrichment," and there they "learn" those things which keep them quarantined from their friends. If they don't learn these things, they take the same course again and are put into "writing laboratories." They receive certificates instead of diplomas. They do not go to college. They never pass GO or collect $200.

The implication of all this is that there is something divinely ordained about the steps or stages in which writing is taught so that one thing must come before another. I have heard more than one teacher say about grade school children that they can't learn to write poems until they learn to write prose, by which it can only be meant they are not allowed to. (Everyone knows the horrors of the corresponding stages in reading with the hideously "graded" primers.) In fact, of course, it was not God but the schools that devised the system whereby students had to "learn grammar" before they could "progress" to Edgar Allan Poe, and to "learn" a story and a poem by Poe before set loose on *Romeo and Juliet*. The schools were organized in given ways—seventh grade-eighth grade-ninth grade, "basic"-regular-advanced—and the teaching of writing and our presumptions about the learning of writing were made to fit these organizations.

Now no school system would admit to this, but they only defend and do not really deny that it is true. The defenses all insist that schools are not this mechanized at all and in fact allow for a good deal of "creativity" or "originality" on the part of the students. But nothing is more rigidly controlled than the time and place for such creativity. Creative spelling or hand-writing, of course, is out entirely; creative writing is approved of at a fairly early stage as long as it isn't used where facts are called for, and right down through high school and college creative writing is kept strictly apart from that other kind. The "creative" student who approves of the work he is given usually has some leeway; the "creative" student who objects is usually firmly, if regretfully, tossed into some group that includes those who can't spell or won't hand in work or are otherwise "un-teachable." When I was in school, everyone still had to read *Silas Marner* in the tenth grade. I wasn't creative, or perhaps just not smart enough to read it at all, but I was a good enough student to avoid the fate of a boy who told the teacher he wouldn't write on *Silas Marner* because it wasn't worth writing on. Thinking *Silas Marner* not worth writing on in the tenth grade was not the least original, but saying so was, and was creative too. This was, in fact, the only time I can remember in all my years in school that someone implied the other books we read in school might be worth reading by saying that one was not. Of course the teacher could not tell him why *Silas Marner* was indeed worth reading; in any event, she missed one of the few chances our class gave her to conduct a conversation not totally banal or inane, a conversation that could not have been easy or even satisfying but that could have been a better defense of teaching English in school than any I heard as a student, before or after.

No, the point about originality carries no weight, as any student knows. All "that" is fitted in "where it belongs," and the implication is that someone, probably the teacher, knows at every step of the way, throughout each class, each unit, each semester, where everything belongs. *This* is "how we do a re-search paper," and *that* is "taught in our journalism class," and "expressive" students who don't say they won't write on *Silas Marner* are allowed to "take creative writing." You can occa-sionally catch even good teachers saying they "can't teach" Shakespeare to "regular students" but that "it goes very well with the students in Advanced Placement."

This strict organization, regimentation, and mechanization of the teaching and learning of English is only a part of the more general processes of systemization which have accompanied democracy and urban technology. What seems demanded of the citizenry is a rather high level of competence in the reading, writing, and speaking of various jargons. It is not only in high schools and colleges that the nigh endless compartmentalization of "communication skills" takes place. People learn to write television scripts and commercials in one school and to write manuals for engineers, questionnaires and reports for bureaucrats, learned articles for learned journals, news stories and editorials, in other schools or courses. People are "trained" in such writing, and the training can range from a week's cram course to enable policemen to fill out reports to five years' training in graduate school in writing specialized and almost unreadable articles. Everywhere one turns, then, writing is something that is taught as a learnable skill involving set and repeatable patterns.

Perhaps the most obvious sign of this systemization and insistence on competence is in the implicit equation made between "right" and "good" or between "correct" and "excellent." No one, I think, openly states such an equation, but most teachers and, therefore, most students operate in fact as though such an equality existed. It is easier, one quickly sees, to operate in the classroom and much easier to test students if correctness is made equivalent to excellence. Time can be spent on such things as: how to write an introductory paragraph, how to take notes for a research paper, how to prepare footnotes, how to decode the teacher's marks in the margin, how to use a dictionary. The implication of such teaching for all but the most extraordinary student is simple: If I learn these processes I will be considered good or even excellent. Few teachers try to say what is good about a good introductory paragraph, and certainly no one asks what would happen if a paper had no introductory paragraph at all. "A good introductory paragraph clearly tells the reader what is to follow," and so on. Which is to say, an introduction introduces something and a good introduction is also clear. Which is to say nothing whatsoever. Which is to say to the average student: "Don't ask questions."

Thus, both student and teacher accept roles which take their intelligence at much less than full potential value by reducing their subject to something close to the level of learning how to drive a car. There is something horrible about all this. We all know that teachers who repeatedly fail students who can't spell or don't write complete sentences present a ghastly spectacle, though perhaps only an English teacher who listens a good deal to his colleagues knows how widespread is this mechanical and intellectually bankrupt practice. We all like to think we are enlightened and that we have moved beyond the brutal pedagogical practices of other generations and centuries. The whole thrust of the movement known as progressive education was directed against rote and mechanical learning, which equated correctness and excellence, incorrectness and failure. No English teacher on any level would cheerfully admit to contributing to a climate in which competence is the highest possible goal. Our air should be brighter, fresher, easier for all to breathe. Yet it is not. Students really do think English teachers are purveyors of rules and symbols, and it does not matter if the students are right or wrong about "us," because if they *think* this, the damage has been done.

The best way I know to explain how this situation came about is to imagine the early career of a good, solid, not terribly exciting teacher of English. Let us imagine this teacher obtains whatever degree he needs from a university and starts out in a college. He teaches nine to twelve hours a week. To the high-school teacher these seem like ideal working conditions, but there is no fun in them. The average class in composition has twenty-five students, and these students are asked to write some kind of theme or essay every other week. When he begins, the teacher finds these three or four daily classes the equivalent of three or four major surgical operations: each is exploratory, dangerous, and exhausting, and people who have never done it have no idea what hard work it is to teach carefully and skillfully for fifty minutes. Class preparation helps, but usually just to settle the stomach and brains, not to make class any easier. On top of this, the student papers must be read, early in the morning, late at night, five or six at a time between classes. Many students have trouble with the mechanics of writing, and most teachers find they often do not improve as time goes by, no matter how hard or diligently their papers are corrected. For many teachers, after a few years, it becomes easy to give up really reading the papers and instead to look for mistakes, to grade on the number of mistakes made, with a few points thrown in for something called "the ideas." If all a teacher has to do is to circle misspelled words, write "fragment" whenever he spots an incomplete sentence, and advise the student to consult the handbook on writing conclusions, he has cut at least in half the time and energy it takes to read a paper. Soon the teacher of composition begins to think that students who can't write complete sentences must learn how to do so before they can be allowed to analyze plays or poems or to do whatever is next in the hierarchy of steps established by the school. Two, three, or five years spent in this way leads an intelligent, well-meaning teacher into doing exactly what he objected to in his own teachers when he was on the other side of the desk. Teaching composition has been reduced to pointing out mistakes, and learning has been reduced to the avoiding of error. The "good" paper has few marks on it, and the "bad" paper is covered with red marks. When the mechanically correct paper goes without much comment, students who seek to make peace with their teachers learn to write mechanically correct papers and have done.

Most teachers in literature courses reverse the process, but the result is the same or worse. Papers are summarily corrected: Few comments are made along the way, all but glaring compositional errors are overlooked, and a brief comment, usually very general, about "the ideas" is all the student gets besides his grade. The only requirement for obtaining a C or better on a "ten-page paper" is that the paper be ten pages long and inoffensive.

It finally seems easier for both teacher and student of composition to let the matter of writing become a mechanical matter. To repeat, no one ever says this is what happens, and both teachers and students learn little rhetorical routines to camouflage the fact; students are told they must "get beneath the surface" or "be thorough," and most students may even think that is what they are doing. The system needs no such justification, however, because it is really self-justifying. As long as there are good students and bad students, teachers can feel that they are making real distinctions: this paper here is clearly incompetent, so it gets a D or an E, but that paper there is perfectly competent, however dull, and gets anything ranging from a C to an A. Some bad students do make fewer mechanical mistakes as time goes on if they care enough about getting a decent grade, and often some merely competent writers become really competent. It looks like worthwhile human activity.

But it isn't, and the major purpose of this book is to suggest a few other ways in which writing can be thought about. I would hate to have anyone think, however, that my lack of sympathy for the way English is generally taught and learned means that I am not interested in what is usually called "good English." I am, in those ways I know how to be, and although this is not a book about how to write good English, I would like to make a general statement about good English, correct usage, and the like. It is an immensely complex subject when considered thoroughly, and all that can be said here is mundane and practical.

The Point About "Good English"

"Good English" became a concern of our culture when English became a subject to be taught. If you think of the matter that way, you probably can also make a good guess as to when that was and why.

Earlier—let us not worry about when—most writers gave themselves a good deal of freedom in matters of spelling, grammar, and usage, and they gave this freedom to themselves because there was no one else to give it to them or to take it from them. No writer at any time has ever felt he could write as he pleased or that he need pay no attention to the way others had written or were writing; all writing must be intelligible to be anything. But if you spent some time looking through a book like Abbott's *A Shakespearean Grammar*, you would see that Shakespeare's sense of what he could and could not do with words was never something he formulated and was also constantly changing. At that time, and for a long time afterward, few people wrote at all, and those who did were usually presumed to be what we would call "educated," or even "gentlemen." With the arrival of mass printing and democracy (the two go hand-in-hand), however, everyone began to be taught to read and write because it was possible for everyone to learn, and it was considered important that everyone do so. People began at that time to worry about "correct" English because they were worrying about the "incorrect" English used by many people. This meant, for instance, that dialects tended to be suppressed, and eventually most speech, like most writing, was in some standard English. This meant, too, that personal idiosyncrasies were no longer regarded as idiosyncrasies at all but as aberrations or deviations from the norm. When a people seek universal literacy, as they do in both England and America, some standards of correctness will be formulated so that everyone will know what is expected of him in matters of usage. In speech, a good deal more freedom is always allowed because the person spoken to is right there, and he can object if he doesn't like or doesn't understand what he hears. But writing that isn't personal in the way speech is, writing that isn't letters or diaries or something written strictly for oneself, presumes an impersonal and unknown audience who will understand only standard correct English.

People debate this matter a good deal, and it would take more space than I can give just to summarize the different arguments. The two major points of view can be noted, however. The first states that any language is simply what it is at any period in time, so that the task for the student of language is simply to describe and analyze what is there. The second states that the language cannot be truly expressive unless some constant concern for precision and grace is expressed by people like English teachers, magazine editors, and dictionary makers. Proponents of the first position think that those who hold the second position are snobs and reactionaries trying to keep the language static or fixed. Proponents of the second position think that those who hold the first are philistines and boors who do not see what resources of the language are lost when no one concerns himself with standards of good and correct English. Following this debate is rather like watching a tennis game: the head moves back and forth, the opponents take turns winning points, and the spectator feels very much like a spectator. As always, there is much to be said on both sides, and fortunately we do not have to try to settle the matter here, where the problem to be faced is more practical: what should the average student in an English course do about the matter?

The first thing to realize about what are sometimes called "the rules of good English" is that there are almost no absolute laws, hard, fast, fixed, and agreed upon by everyone. But some things are agreed upon by so many people that they might as well be absolute. Most of these are matters of grammar, that is, of the mechanics whereby words are inflected and conjugated and made to fit so as to form idiomatic phrases and sentences. "I am" is correct and "I are" is incorrect, "The book belongs to him" is correct and "The book belongs to his" is incorrect. Subjects must agree, in most cases, with modifying adjectives and with verbs. Verb tenses cannot be confused—"When I *was* walking down the street, he *is* coming to meet me" is incorrect. But rather than fuss about the matter of correctness, let us say that most people will object if you write in ignorance or defiance of what we all think of as correct grammatical usage. Some of these matters of grammar simply have to be learned, but most of them we learn when we learn to speak and long before we ever write. "His book" is what we hear around us, not "he book," so that is what we learn.

It is impossible to say where the rock-bottom rules of grammar leave off and matters of usage, coherence, or nicety begin, but because most people learn what is truly rock-bottom as they first learn the language, the problems that arise in writing usually are not these but ones on which there is widespread but far from universal agreement. Often teachers seem as outraged about what they consider violations of these rules as they do about mistakes in the more fundamental grammars of the language. For instance, "I have no money" is good English, but "I got no money" is not, when "got" is used to denote possession rather than gaining possession. "He couldn't help but fail" and "He couldn't hardly see" are both double negatives and usually considered poor English, though both are, like "I got no money," often heard in everyday speech. There are guidelines about the proper use of "like" and "as," such that the phrasing of the advertisement for Winston cigarettes, "Winston

[25]

tastes good like a cigarette should," is generally considered incorrect. "The problem centers around money" and "In terms of houses, this is a small street" are marked defective by most teachers. "That is an uncomfortable chair" is perfectly good English, but "We looked over a dizzy cliff" is not, though it is not easy to see why this is so. I become annoyed with people who use "quote" or "potential" as nouns, or "contact" as a transitive verb, or "minimize" or "finalize" as verbs of any kind, or words invented by *Time* magazine. Other teachers may find these usages anything ranging from acceptable to swell. Most students learn rather early in their careers that there are all manner of problems in the English language which they do not understand and which have never been explained to them. They also learn that one teacher stresses one thing and another teacher something quite different, and so the students finally stop trying to understand everything and simply find out what each teacher likes or does not like.

It would be nice to think I or someone else could suddenly explain the intricacies and complexities of good English. But if I could, I would also be setting myself up as a target for someone else with a quite different explanation of what constitutes good English. I can and shall explain some things I happen to consider important, and I'll try to say why I think they're important, but that is probably as much as I can do. If there is any rule about good English, it is that you should not do anything which you know to be contrary to generally agreed upon standards without having a good reason for doing so. There is nothing sillier than the sight of someone trying to display a new device he's seen or thought up when he doesn't know what it's good for. Some students, when they discover that Jack London or Thomas Wolfe failed an English course, or that Faulkner has some sentences which seem endless, think they should, or even must, go out and break any and all rules they ever learned in the name of free expression or the like. If automatic teaching is bad, automatic rejection of that teaching is no better. The student who finds himself with a teacher who insists on "the rules of good English" need not feel in bondage. Almost anything anyone wants to say can be said in good English. The student whose teacher flunks students for more than one sentence fragment or comma fault per paper is in for a dreary course, no question about it. But he can still write complete and properly subordinated sentences. There is probably no good reason not to.

Teachers can be oppressive, but so, too, can students be tiresome, especially when they try to play games with teachers and with good English just to see if they can. Let me offer an example. I am making this one up, so I may not have caught the right tone, but it seems to me that every now and then I am given something like this to comment on:

> The great unwashed washed over the pavement down into the by now muffled roar of passing subways under M Street. The next wave would leave my world free for six precious minutes while I could discover if my mind was going in circles or squares today or if it would hop along in hexagons and badly inscribed whorls and dart down holes marked wrong way do not enter.

I always feel that the student who writes like this is saying to me: "See, teacher, I am of the NOW generation, you are old and have brown mud in your veins." It is a dare which is no fun either to take or to reject. It also is usually meant as an implied threat: "If you reject this I will laugh at you; if you accept this I will say you are clumsy and like all the others over thirty who try to groove by imitating their youngers and betters." In any event, I do not feel the writer is trying to tell me something but is instead playing low-risk games, in which case I want to tell the student to stop playing games.

So, it is important to have a good reason when you are going to do something you know runs counter to your sense of good English. But supposing you don't know that what you are doing is wrong, and after a teacher circles it and makes some explanation that does not explain, you still do not know what is wrong. People "should know better," perhaps. Still, to take one small example, I constantly come upon sentences like the following: "He didn't like Tess too much, so he didn't care what happened to her"; "None of the people thought there was too much point in obeying King Richard, so they did not object when some of the nobles rebelled"; "She knew it was wrong to drink so much because she didn't know him too well yet." I wearily circle the "too" in each case, and perhaps write something like

[27]

"very" in the margin whenever I find sentences like these, but I have few illusions that when I do so it will make any difference. The student almost certainly does not know why I am objecting to his use of "too," and probably all but the fullest explanation will not help. The fault concerns the use of "too" with a negative; for example, in its simplest form, "I don't like my coffee too hot." That and the sentences above verge on nonsense because "too" means excess, more than is right or possible or safe or healthy. By definition of "too," no one likes his coffee *too* hot, or his steak *too* rare, no citizen can see *too* much point in obeying the king. In "He didn't like Tess too much . . ." and ". . . she didn't know him too well yet," as in all other examples above, what is meant is not "too" but "very" or something similar.

The student who looks at my circle of his "too" and reads my "very" in the margin lives in a world where such usage generally passes without comment. He knows I am in the minority of people who care about the matter, and I know it too. My advice to the student is always this: if I or any other teacher seems to you courteous and interested in your welfare and civilization, pay attention, listen, ask questions, or at least do not ever commit the fault again in his presence; if it is feasible, ask him what is wrong. On the other hand, if I or any other teacher who objects to the way you use English seems interested in using his greater learning as a club over you, pay attention to the comment and ignore the teacher; find out from someone else what is wrong with "I don't like my coffee too hot"; find out somehow, and hope that if the person explains the point well you will begin to see that the English language seeks to make sense rather than rules.

But no one knows all the sense that the English language makes or can make, or all the nonsense it can make. The more sense you can make it make, the better you will write. Some of this is a matter of rules, and a great deal of it is about what the rules are about, but you do not have to think of writing as a matter of laws and edicts. I will be speaking about this matter from time to time throughout the book; for now let it be said that the subject of good English is a subject, not a list of unexplainable rules.

*The Way "Good English" and
"Good Writing" and "Good
Students" Are Teachable. And
What Is Wrong*

There are two very good reasons why "good English," "good writing," and "good students" are teachable, even by fairly ordinary teachers. The first is that, in the case of the majority of students, most of the work has already been done for the teachers. The second is that teachers have enough authority over students that they can get a minimal response from almost everyone and then scale their expectations down so that minimal response seems like a great deal.

Most students learn a written English that is different from but generally not at odds with their spoken English, so even those teachers who seek to teach very formal writing under laboratory conditions do not work in a total vacuum. Students who grow up hearing and speaking American English hear standard good English or something like it all their lives, and so, to move from speech to writing, need only be taught those artificial steps whereby writing becomes formal. Even so, when these students feel pressed to write very differently from the way they speak, they get into weird habits in their writing. But those students—in this country they are mostly blacks— who grow up hearing and speaking something different from standard English, are almost unteachable by most teachers, because the teachers can no longer rely on the original habits of home and street to do their work for them. The suburban white child often hears, "I don't like my coffee too hot," and so he says it; the ghetto black child hears not only "I don't like my coffee too hot," but "Have you got 25 cent?" and "I'm gonna beat up on you" and "I got no money," so he says them. All these usages are really equally right or equally wrong, but because the whites have the power, they tolerate "I don't like my coffee too hot" with shocking equanimity and stigmatize "I got no money" with equally shocking equanimity. When teachers insist they cannot teach twentieth-century students eighteenth-century English, when we protest that the language is a living language, what we mean is that standard language is living for

[29]

those who have power. For those who are powerless it lives only outside of school. As a result, many teachers will declare students unteachable, when what they really mean is that some students speak (and write) so differently from themselves as to live in a different world, and that they cannot be bothered to do anything other than try to make all students toe the same standard English line. In the normal college course in composition this is not a serious problem because, by the time most students get to college, be they black, white, or "other," they have learned to play ball with their teachers in ways I described in an earlier section of this chapter. But all this means is that the barbaric usages of the majority are allowed and the usages of some minorities are called barbaric.

The second reason that good English is teachable is more relevant here, because it focuses on the means whereby it is taught to everyone. I have said that good English or any other kind of English is generally explainable, but also that it is often difficult and time-consuming and apparently unprofitable to do so. As a result, teaching, in most situations that involve good English as a subject, only duplicates in the student that which is known by the teacher, and it does this usually by a simple assertion of authority. If I know that "I don't like my coffee too hot" is nonsense, I can try to explain why it is to any student who uses the phrase. But that is hard work, and I can also simply say to the student "Do that again and I'll get you." This is generally how it is done, and as a result, to most students wrong English usage comes to seem like wrong answers in other subjects: "I can't hardly help it" is wrong the way "Andrew Jackson fought at the Alamo" is wrong and the way $4/5 \times 7/8 = 7/9$ is wrong. Students learn about these wrong answers by being corrected and are made to find out the right answer under the threat of some kind of reprisal. The first is a grammatical error, the second is a factual error, the third is a computational error, but most students know them simply as wrong answers and seek ways of not making the same mistake again: "I can hardly help it"; "Andrew Jackson fought at the battle of New Orleans"; $4/5 \times 7/8 = 7/10$.

Most people do so much of their learning in school in just this way, that often they come to think this is all learning is, can be, or should be. In high school and college, most teachers try to disguise how much rote learning or memory work they are asking of their students, but a good student knows that simple kinds of learning will get him through most situations. Everyone knows it is easier to remember certain facts and right ways to do things if he also understands what is involved; but still, remembering is the goal. The examination system seeks this kind of learning, and most courses operate on examinations. The fifth-grader will be asked, "What did the Emancipation Proclamation do?" and he will be expected to answer, "It freed the slaves." The tenth-grader will be asked, "Which slaves were freed by the Emancipation Proclamation?" and he will be expected to answer, "The slaves in the states of the Confederacy." The senior in college will be asked, "Why did Lincoln issue the Emancipation Proclamation?" and he will be expected to answer, "To encourage slave uprisings in the southern states. It was a military and political move, not a moral one," and so forth. But the process by which one learns answers to these questions is the same. To move from true-false questions to the twenty-minute essay is to advance only in the length of the answer required.

Students are, of course, encouraged to think that an English paper asks more of a student than a rote answer. In an English paper he is not asked to repeat or rehash someone else's ideas but to express his own—that, at least, is the official rhetoric about the matter. But in fact, students learn to write English papers as automatically as they learn to answer questions about the Emancipation Proclamation. Both teachers and students try to hide this fact, but they don't really succeed in fooling themselves or each other. Students learn "good English" and "English papers" so they could almost write them in their sleep.

Three Specimen Papers

A class was recently asked to read an essay by Philip Wylie called "A Specimen American Institution," which serves as one chapter in his *Generation of Vipers*. The specimen American institution is the public school system, and Wylie attacks it wildly. It is the kind of writing that seeks violent protest or loud hurrahs from its readers. The student was asked to quote a passage from the essay and then comment on it, not to repeat or rehash someone else's ideas, but to express his own.

—I—

The school is an organism which teaches reading, writing, and arithmetic. It does that so the pupil can communicate. These accomplishments should also be taught so the student can think, but few schools have stumbled upon that notion of education. A thinking child would not think much of a school which would upset the system.

Schools nowadays do not just teach thinking for communication, though they do an admirable job in that field as is evidenced by the amount of writing in circulation today. In addition to plays, historical romances, and biographies, there are scientific and nonfictional essays and books on the state of the world, economics, government, technology, and any subject that you might name. Children are being taught to think in schools today. If, as Wylie points out, a thinking child would not think much of school, this can only expose the poor job of teaching done in that particular school. A child who has been taught to think can reason beyond the temporary hardships of attending classes each day. He can reason out that a good education is an extremely valuable commodity. An educated man today commands a high salary on the open market. Many of the people, today considered successful, have college degrees. The businessman today doesn't get by with just incentive and luck. Instead, he hires the smartest, most well-educated people, and he acts on the basis of their advice.

Contrary to Wylie's view, it is the nonthinking student who upsets today's system. While the thinker completes his education and becomes a useful and active member of society, the nonthinker becomes a sponge, a leech, a hazard to society. The nonthinker will drop out of school in search of a better life, but there are no good jobs open for him, because he doesn't have the necessary education. So he becomes dissatisfied with one bad job and moves to another, and he eventually quits altogether. He may start drinking and he may collapse, but mostly he whines that he didn't have a fair chance in life. Consider the summer riots. Many of the looters and snipers aren't thinking and don't see they are getting a terrible reputation, making it even difficult for them to escape their squalid environment. They'll only be despised for what they are instead of pitied for what they might have been.

Perhaps twenty years ago Wylie's description of the school system would have been accurate. Today it is exactly opposed to reality. The system and the country want thinking people, for they help society, and that is the desire of the entire organization known as man.

This is not an elegantly written paper, but its small clumsinesses are not its major fault. It is a good example of a "learned" or "canned" paper, one that lets itself drift and swirl in and around a few simple notions. Its argument is certainly not very persuasive and is not laden with clarifying examples, but it makes its point all right. As a species of good English, it is never distinguished and never graceful, but it is seldom incompetent.

The key word in the paper is "today"; the word is used seven times, and "nowadays" once. In each case the writer wants to rebuke someone: this is how things are "today," buddy, and how they should be all the time. Today a good education gets one a good job and success, and therefore any thinking student will want a good education. The argument follows the lines set down by advertisements for shampoos and after-shave lotions. There's something about an Aqua-Velva man—not that he uses Aqua-Velva or that for a few minutes after he splashes it on he smells nice, but that he rides motorcycles, surfs, dances, never works, and has his pick of women. He is successful, and the thinking man will use Aqua-Velva, just as in this paper the thinking man will stay in school.

Those who are revolted by this line of argument and who call it smug or conformist or names more harsh never try to remember how compelling an argument this is, in its way. If you want what your society considers success, you must play and want to play society's game and in society's ballpark: in this case, you go to school and do as you're told. If you don't do this, the consequences are potentially fierce: you become a whiner, a drifter, maybe a black rioter who seeks the writer's pity but gains only his contempt. There is neither point nor necessity in objecting to the position taken by this paper. What is disastrously wrong is the almost total predictability of its motion: "In addition to plays, historical Romances, and biographies, there are many scientific and nonfictional essays and books on the state of the world, economics, government, technology, and any subject that you might name." Ask yourself who that sounds like. It reminds me of the memorized or recorded speech of a librarian who is offering her monologue to a straggling group of visitors. To this writer, all subjects are of equal importance and all books are of equal value; what is important is that they be produced in great quantity and that anyone be able to say anything he wants in them. It is to the vast productive capacity of America that this writer owes his allegiance, and to its "democratic" acceptance of all subjects. "The mind," said Alexander Pope of such minds, "in metaphysics at a loss, wanders in a wilderness of moss." It thinks that books that sell many copies must be good books, and libraries with many volumes must be good libraries; perhaps it thinks corporations with the most assets and universities with the most students are best too.

Everything this writer thinks of as belonging inside the system is "good," and everything outside is "bad." What lies outside are the failures, and these can be identified either by their unproductiveness or by their inability or refusal to work hard: bad guys complain, loot, riot, and confuse the defective school system of twenty years ago with the efficient system of Today. But merely to identify the writer's ethic is not adequate condemnation; his general position could be defended much better than is done here. What is wrong is that living contentedly inside the system has blinded the writer. He knows no distinctions, sees no need to ask questions. All thinking is subsumed under the easy rubric of success and conformity, so that it does not matter what one thinks about, or how well. What can go on in a mind that thinks *that?* Only the semblance of mental activity.

How should a teacher speak to this writer? It is hard to flatter, persuade, or shock such a man, because he knows all the answers already. He believes in technical proficiency, and so he would probably welcome correction of his mechanical mistakes —that's what teachers are for, and such criticism is "constructive criticism." But a teacher who tried either to attack his ethic or to point out the slovenly habits of mind it has engendered in his case would be in danger of being called some kind of non-thinker, a cynic perhaps, or a sorehead, someone who, by implication, is taking out his failure to be a success in the system by punishing those who work happily inside it. This student's categories for people and activities are easy, predictable, and almost impossible to change.

Our second paper certainly seems quite different from the first.

—II—

The goals of our society are such that only the less attractive and the less aggressive remain to teach—the social leftovers.

Let me assume that I have had a normal educational background, and on this assumption, I will base some statements about the attractiveness and aggressiveness of public school teachers.

First, however, I must distinguish between primary and high-school teachers. Grades one through six are taught by very nice, middle-aged ladies who think very little or not at all. They are definitely not social leftovers; rather, PTA meetings and bridge clubs are packed with such cattle. But high-school teachers are something else again.

Social studies teachers try to sustain the manners of English kings but also have the look and smell of giraffes. English teachers are usually women, and they always seem to employ their male students as props. Mathematics instructors possess breath so noxious that it makes one shrivel prunelike upon their approach. These facts must be accepted in their disgusting reality.

Those few teachers who are fairly presentable care too little about their jobs to correct assignments promptly or keep up with discoveries in their fields. If they were not sheltered by the school system, they could not survive in the day-to-day competition of the business community.

But why are these misfits the molders of American youth? There are many competent members of our society who are dedicated to teaching. Their work is done on the campuses of colleges and universities. Only the leftovers go into high schools.

[35]

There are many more potential teachers of high caliber working in good-paying technological jobs. Low pay and lack of prestige discourage these imaginative and energetic people from working in the public schools. If we can assume all this is true, I now arrive at my main point.

Materialism is not as important as people think. The sense of appreciation and of being recognized that go along with a higher salary is the most important consideration. As matters stand, the average history or English major is laughed at because everybody knows the "flunky" is going to become a public school teacher, while many of his contemporaries will take higher-paying engineering or business positions.

If a school system started paying teachers salaries as good as those in the business world, things would improve. Many oppose increasing teachers' salaries just to raise their standard of living. But salary affects the sense of appreciation, however, and so my solution is the only course.

This paper received from its grader a much higher mark than did the first, and although it is better in some respects, it isn't clearly superior at all. The writer of the first paper seems to disagree with Wylie and to look on him as one of those "outsiders" who whine about the way the system works. The writer of the second paper seems to agree with Wylie and falls into the spirit of the attack. But the disagreement between the two writers is superficial. What neither would easily recognize is that it is no more difficult to be a cheap cynic than it is to be a cheap conformist, and in this case the two are closely allied. Both students accept the validity of labels like "conformist" and "cynic" in describing large groups of people, and both write to conform to their labels: "Grades one through six are taught by very nice middle-aged ladies who think very little or not at all. They are definitely not social leftovers; rather, PTA meetings and bridge clubs are packed with such cattle." The writer assumes his position is unpopular, and so his tone is aggressive. He seems to ask for simple condemnation: "young punk"; or else simple approval: "hurrah." He picks easy targets, and targets about which he (it is a man writing, to be sure) is sufficiently ignorant, so his use of terms like "cattle" can express all he knows about them.

If his teacher objects to his tone, he has a built-in reply:

English teachers are leftovers. For this man believes as strongly and simply in Today as does the first writer: teachers should be presentable and not smell bad, they should be up-to-date in their fields (whatever that means), they should resemble businessmen and engineers who really have to be smart. In order, therefore, to make them less like giraffes and more like chairmen of the board, we should pay them more. His scorn of the teacher with bad breath is like the first writer's scorn of the rioter, and both derive their habits of mind from television advertisements: the man isn't with it.

By calling a paper like this simple I mean mostly that the reader knows what it is going to be like after one or two sentences. This writer, like the first one, let Wylie press a button in him, and then he came out with his spiel. Each learns his point as an argument, as a conversational counter to be used whenever the button is pushed. All writing is made to resemble writing one might do for a debate, and the average student can make many speeches on a whole variety of subjects. He can talk about the effectiveness or the ineffectiveness of the United Nations; about the wickedness of black rioters or the need for social reconstruction in our cities; about the benefits or the special ills of democracy; about the necessity or inequity of our laws about guns, narcotics, zoning, or helmets for drivers of motorcycles. In a debate one is of necessity simple-minded, because the job of the debater is not to see things steadily and wholly but to offer only those arguments and examples which support his point. It is often thought that debates encourage broad-mindedness, but if they do they also seem to achieve simple-mindedness.

Before looking more thoroughly at the kind of paper represented in the previous examples, let us look at our third example as a way of seeing why the first two have become so acceptable in our schools that an attack on them almost seems like an attack on democracy itself.

—III—

In these days of war [he is writing about World War II], *patriots are busy saying that the debunking which has been mod-*

estly attempted in the last few decades has so soured and spoiled
the souls of the young that they have no patriotism at all, no
eagerness to die for their land, and no earnest will to fight for
freedom. Of the young soldiers, there is no use to speak. They
no longer have any choice. But the indictment squarely fits mil-
lions of civilians. It fits not because of honest iconoclasm, however, but because of the failure of everybody—the educators, the
intellectuals, the debunkers, and the sleazy people themselves—
to hunt up and substitute real values for the false ones that were
taken away by the debunking.

In the past generation "real values" have been abandoned for
the sake of "false values." This awful event could be attributed to
what is termed "debunking." Wylie illustrates debunking through
his giving up of sincere patriotism.

In recent years many events .characterize the disloyalty of one
to his country. The recent craze of burning draft cards reveals
Wylie's point. These boys, supposed men, protest their country's
ideals by burning their cards. Mostly this act has weak grounds
and seldom achieves much except strife. Another case where patriotism is doubtful is people burning the flag. It seems evident
the sacred liberties and institutions given us by the founding
fathers are in danger of attack.

The hippie situation which is presently confronting us in our
own area shows "there is no earnest will to fight for freedom."
Although they are advocating love and peace instead of war,
what are the hippies doing? They are sitting at home making
specimens of themselves and biting the hands that feed them.

Due to the present struggle in Vietnam, thousands of men are
being drafted today. Before he is taken into service, everyone must
pass a physical examination. And a great number of people are
deliberately trying to flunk this test. The "eagerness to die for
their land" seems to be shot.

Wylie explains that there is no need for people to speak out,
because they no longer have any choice. Of course, their efforts
are in vain. Why? Because up to now they have burned flags
and destroyed their draft cards, have riotous demonstrations and
even use underhanded methods. Of course no one will listen to
their outcries. Our country is built upon many concepts, including patriotism. To live in such a world, a certain amount of conformity is demanded. Here patriotism is required.

As the turmoil in the area of education and schools continues,
we find ourselves, once again, in a destructive war of liberalism

versus conservatism. If educators, intellectuals, debunkers, and sleazy people would cooperate and mold their ideas so we can all revert back to the "real values," our needed patriotism could be restored.

As Coleridge once said about a line of Thomas Gray's, this has almost as many faults as it has words. There can be no point in describing them, and the teacher who tries could only overwhelm himself and the student with anguish and despair. The more one looks at the paper, the more incoherent it becomes. It is in the name of this paper that the first two escape without much comment or even get some praise. The system has failed with the third writer, who is blithely unaware, not just of the commonplace quality of his mind, but of his unfamiliarity with the English language: "The hippie situation which is presently confronting us in our own area shows 'there is no earnest will to fight for freedom.' " A description of all that is wrong, vague, or stupid about that sentence would take at least 500 words; writers of textbooks on English normally have to search for a long time before finding something as inept.

Teachers who give failing grades fail this paper, while the first two receive anything from C to A. If asked to defend such grades, any teacher could do so, as though that were the end of the matter; they too can commit the fallacy of the arguable proposition, to which we will come in a while. Any system or scale of values that can justify itself is perpetuated, so students continue to write papers like these three, and teachers continue to comment on them and grade them, knowing justifications are available for all moves made on both sides. It is a game played in every school in the country, and it is not becoming less popular. The first paper gets a C and complaints about its smugness, the second paper gets a B or better and complaints about its minor mistakes, the third paper gets a D or worse, and a sigh.

My inclination would be to give the first paper a C, the second a C plus, and the third a C minus, though of course depending on my mood, the second might get as high as a B and the third as low as a D. But the closer together the grades come, the clearer is the principle that however great are the differences between the incompetent boring paper and the competent boring paper, both are boring. Were my job to train these three writers to write or edit reports for a management consulting firm, or to check on applicants for the Foreign Service or for positions as night watchmen, then the situation would be different. In the tough, real, competitive business and engineering world of Today envisaged by all three writers, the first two could be very successful, while the third probably should be encouraged to join the PTA or the bridge club so deplored by the second. But as a teacher of English composition I can serve no useful function in my society unless I tell all three writers that they write like machines—some are well-oiled and adjusted, some imperfectly assembled, but all are machines.

How to Write a Canned Essay

To do this is not at all as hard as is sometimes imagined by those who have never tried or whose training in composition preceded the vogue of the canned essay. Let me start by delineating certain features of the best of the three papers above, and then show how such writing is done.

We begin with the teachers in elementary schools:

> Grades one through six are taught by very nice, middle-aged ladies who think very little or not at all. They are definitely not social leftovers; rather, PTA meetings and bridge clubs are filled with such cattle.

This, we claimed, has a certain vigor, but of an empty, flashy kind. Why "very" sweet and "very" little? Again, does the man know or care what that word means? No, he is simply setting up "nice" against "little or not at all" and putting "very" in to make the switch something he probably thinks of as effective. But the effectiveness of the switch is then deflected or even lost when it turns out that "nice" and "little or not at all" are not really opposed to each other but are, instead, complementary terms describing "cattle." It then becomes clear he does not mean nice at all but probably docile. The writing seems vigorous, then, but really is almost as imprecise as that of the third writer.

[40]

But the intent of the writing is clear. It is, as said above, to elicit a simple response from the reader, either "young punk" or "hurrah," and with writing like this it does not matter what is said as long as those responses are achieved. If the writer had said, "Grades one through six are taught by frustrated women more interested in keeping order than in teaching children," he would, ostensibly, be describing quite a different kind of teacher; but the two sentences aren't really different. The writer isn't interested in teachers in elementary schools at all but in the response he gets from his reader. The moment this becomes clear it is also clear that other and also apparently different sentences would do just as well, and they aren't hard to write at all:

Teachers in grade schools are just glorified babysitters.

Lucky students have one real teacher in grade school; the rest of their teachers stand up front and either plead or shout.

Teachers in grade schools really do teach pupils how to live in our society; they teach the young to submit to their elders and to dream of the day when they can have such power.

In all cases the writer is saying to his reader, who is a teacher: "I challenge you to reject my attack on your union. Agree with me and you betray your own." The reason such writing is very easy is that the actual words aren't important.

For that reason it can help little to reply to this writer, "Be more specific," or "Give examples," or "Is this true of all teachers?" He can be a good deal more specific, in the sense that he is specific in the next paragraph when he divides high-school teachers into English teachers, math teachers, and history teachers, each with their own identifying insignia. If he were asked to describe one such teacher, he would have no trouble at all. The result might look like this:

Mr. Snowden was tall and very thin and he stooped over his students as though he were picking flowers. He sometimes let a whole term's papers and exams pile up on his desk, and he would still be visible when he sat down behind the pile. He wrote names of books on the board in a thin scrawl no one could read, and then mumbled assignments from these books while still facing the blackboard. The pretty girls in the front row got good grades.

This is specific and not at all hard to write. I made it up simply by finding details which corresponded to the desired tone of scorn and challenge. I never had a teacher like my Mr. Snowden, and never heard of one like him either, but I didn't need to.

What is important, then, in writing a canned essay is what is called "angle," "slant," "point of view," or "gimmick." When one is either very relaxed or in a hurry, one can play the game almost the way one plays Password: one word is easily associated with another, then another and another, until a cluster is built up. Adjectives, especially ones like "great," "very," "large," "tiny," "mostly," "all," and "every," can be added to do some "effective" blocking in, and then prepositions and conjunctions tie the words together "into a whole." It may take a little while to get the hang of it, but once the secret is learned, the rest is easy. Some adults underestimate their own ability to write like this, because they were not trained to describe the virtues of Medicare or the follies of the US space program in a couple of minutes. But most people of student age can do it. The most overwhelming proof of this in my experience is the English Composition Achievement Test given by the Educational Testing Service, the major scholastic testing organization in this country. During the test, up to 150,000 students are asked to write a twenty-minute essay on a topic they have never seen before, and the Educational Testing Service is very proud that this part of their battery of exams for high-school seniors applying to college is not graded by machine. Instead, high-school and college teachers meet to read and grade these essays. Those making up the question try to catch the students just enough off guard so they cannot fall back on something they have learned in school. One year, for instance, students were asked to comment on the statement in Shaw's *Man and Superman:*

> The reasonable man adapts himself to the world: the unreasonable one persists in trying to adapt the world to himself. Therefore, all progress depends on the unreasonable man.

I remember that when I first read that quotation and the brief question following, I thought that here was something students could not reply to automatically, because Shaw's statement seemed to run counter to their usual thinking. But I, like the examiners, underestimated the students' ability to outfox their elders, and so sat for a week reading part of the 100,000 essays, most of which resembled the three papers discussed above. Some students are terrific at this, and in twenty minutes they can read the question and then write a competent essay of up to 500 words. To read such papers is to marvel at the quickness and fluidity some people possess. Such writers, one presumes, are destined for great success, as long as they go on believing that the success they want lies in the control of such talent. Others do less well but still can manage 150 words of vaguely connected complete sentences in very little time. Those who have become terrified of the process, or those who have not learned how to work it, stutter, slide, write incomplete and incoherent sentences. There are enough in each of these categories so that the examiners can confidently grade the papers after they get used to the usual spread. To them and to the students, the message of such an examination is clear: write fast, and worry about nothing else at all but getting your notions in some apparent order.

The trouble with such a system is not really that it is wrong, but that the people who work it soon believe that it is the only way to operate. At the grading sessions for this twenty-minute essay I meet English teachers from all over the country who feel that, in some small way, we are keeping English up in the democracy. I meet, also, others who dislike the whole process but who, like me, go along with it and pretend that competence and excellence are the same thing instead of being, as they are in some cases, at odds with each other. Suppose a paper starts out to say something really interesting but gets no further than the middle of one paragraph. How many interesting sentences can one write in twenty minutes, anyway, on a subject not of one's own choosing? The grader is stuck. He can mark it down on the grounds that three sentences do not a paper make, or he can sneakily mark it up and hope that the promising sentences he sees before him really are a sign of distinction in the writer and not just a slightly different twist on a standard variation. It is easy to become absurdly lenient about almost anything that is

[43]

different from the preceding ten or twenty papers and to begin to see high quality that is not really there.

But these papers are fairly uncommon. By far the greatest majority are written by good students or mediocre students or bad students, and can be graded along the scale implied by such terms. These students' efforts, like the English courses in high school they grow out of and like the English courses in college they lead into, are disheartening. It takes practice to make one fluent, and a kind of good teaching too, but it takes very little thought and only moderate willingness to be deluded into thinking that this boring work, which most teachers and students know is boring, is really worth doing.

"Tell Us What You Want, Sir"

Thus far, I'm sure some readers feel, I've managed mostly to sound very superior and knowing, as though I were running down the opposition and had no obligation to introduce my new product. "You don't like English papers and you don't like English teachers. Okay, what do you like?"

A moment similar to this comes in almost every class I've ever taught. I give an assignment, or two, or three. Maybe I give an assignment like the one the writers discussed above were given. I comment, and grade the papers as I said I might do, and give all three varying forms of a C. The writer of the C minus paper is perhaps relieved, because they had told him in high school he didn't write very well and he got Cs in English there. They had also told him college was a lot harder than high school, and here is a C, so maybe he can hack it all right. But the writers of the C and C plus papers are probably angry or confused. They may figure college is sufficiently different from high school, so they will be quiet this time, or even the next, but sooner or later, if they go on writing papers like the ones above, and if they gradually rid their work of small blemishes, and still get Cs, they're going to be sore. One or both are going to protest: "Tell us what you want." If they add a surly "sir," then I know in advance they are not going to like the only answer I can give them: "I have no idea. I can't know what I want until I see something I like."

The person who asks, "What do you want?" assumes that I know what I want when I give out an assignment and that I will measure what I get back against some ideal that I have in my head. Now if I did know what I wanted my students to write, it would be dishonest not to tell them. But the moment I say, "This is what I want you to do," I say also, in effect, "Follow the dots," or "Jump through these hoops," and "Think like me." Here is Philip Wylie, here is what I think of him, now you say what you think. If I do that, any reasonably cautious student is going to trim his sails to my wind. He won't write down exactly what I told him, but he'll sense what I want, and he'll produce it for me. There are a number of names for me if I do this, none of them complimentary; "bully" is perhaps the best.

Look at the following questions:

What is the population of Brazil?

Who is the hero of *A Farewell to Arms?*

How did Newton formulate his laws of motion?

Why did England go to war with Germany in 1939?

Assume you have to explain the essentials of English grammar to someone who knows no English. How would you proceed?

If you look at those questions in order, you might well conclude they get harder or more complicated moving down the list. That is one way of putting the matter. But perhaps it would be better to say that the questioner increasingly is leaving the question of the complexity of the answer up to the answerer. All these questions can be answered simply, and all but perhaps the first can be answered in complex ways. So it isn't the questions themselves that are terribly important but the relationship of questioner to answerer, of teacher to student. If the student assumes that the teacher who asks why England went to war with Germany in 1939 wants only to be told the four reasons he offered in class the day before, then the relationship between the two has become a mechanical one, and so the question can be answered simply and mechanically. If, however, the student thinks the teacher finds this matter quite problematical and worth careful deliberation, then trotting out four or fourteen reasons won't help a bit. The student may know the teacher is an expert on this subject and knows more about World War II than the student will ever know, but the teacher's knowledge or lack of it is unimportant compared to the relationship he seeks or implies with his student.

Not that assignments themselves are unimportant. A well-phrased assignment is a work of art, because it can indicate the frontiers of any given inquiry, the boundaries beyond which a student must feel he is on his own. A poor assignment will, of course, imply that there are no such frontiers: "What is the role of Horatio in Shakespeare's *Hamlet?*" "What does Piggy symbolize in William Golding's *Lord of the Flies?*" "Who are the leaves of grass in Whitman's poem?" A willing and open student must feel some discouragement in the face of such questions, though it isn't really the questions that are discouraging to him but their implications about what the teacher seeks of him. They imply that pat answers will be perfectly acceptable. But even these questions can be transformed so as to yield interesting answers. That isn't often done and it isn't easy to do, and the teacher who wants interesting answers probably will not ask such apparently closed-circuited questions. Better questions than these are better simply because they suggest to the student more ways in which he might say what is most on his mind about the subject.

A number of years ago I gave a course in Shakespeare's history plays. For their first paper the students were asked to read Shakespeare's four earliest histories and to write on them in the light of a lovely and very suggestive quotation from W. B. Yeats about the plays. I was rather pleased with the assignment, but the papers I got back were terrible, and, even worse, I could not discover why. When I turned the papers back, no one said much, and when asked, some students muttered something about not liking the assignment but refused to elaborate. So a year later I gave the same course and thought the quotation from Yeats worth another try. I dressed up the assignment a little more, gave the students ways of avoiding it if they really wanted to, talked briefly about the quotation when I handed out the assignment. But the results were little better. This time, however, I pressed to find out what had gone wrong. I finally got an answer that made me feel a fool for not seeing the trouble earlier. The quotation, which is not really obscure but does seem to imply great familiarity with all Shakespeare's history plays, with English history, and with the "millennial traditions" that Yeats said were passing in the history Shakespeare wrote about, intimidated the students. It was on their first assignment for a new teacher. They all took what seemed to be the simplest way out and tried to act as knowing as they felt Yeats was. In order to do this they had to, or thought they had to, try to psych out Yeats and thereby psych out me. They took Yeats' phrases and interpreted them woodenly, because they did not know quite enough to read them flexibly, and they did not trust me when I said they could ignore them. Thrown at them as it was at the beginning of the term, the assignment led most students to believe that Yeats and I were very highflown creatures and that I was asking them to be that way too. So they tried, in whatever ponderous and mechanical ways they could, to fly high, and so fell, like Icarus, into the sea. It was neither the assignment nor the students that was wrong but the timing of the assignment, given the nature of our relationship at that point. In a later year I gave the same assignment to similar students near the end of the course, and they did beautifully with it.

The best way to establish and maintain truly open and respectful relationships between teachers and students is for the teacher to ask questions to which he does not really know the answer, questions to which there are no good simple answers but many good complex ones. But that is not always possible or practical. Teachers are bound to think they know some things well, else they would not be teachers, and so they are bound to ask questions to which they think they know the best answer. But teachers can do many things with their knowledge besides

[47]

measuring students' ignorance, the most important of which is being flexible about the answers they get to their questions. The key to this flexibility is the ability to suggest to all students that what is important is what they think, not what the teacher thinks. For instance, I have my opinion of Philip Wylie, and I think I know how to convey that opinion; in brief, I think he has been in far too few classrooms to speak as authoritatively as he does. As a teacher, I have been in more classrooms, more often, and under more different conditions, than Wylie—but that is not of crucial importance here. My students, too, have spent a great deal of time in classes and are in many ways experts about schools. Their experience consists not only of their thoughts and feelings about what has happened to them but of all they have seen happening to others, some very much like and some very much unlike themselves.

If, then, I ask a student to respond to some fatuous statement of Philip Wylie's, I must also try to indicate that he does not have to give me a fatuous answer. If he tells me that "children are being taught to think in schools today," I do not have to enter into a debate with him about whether he is right. Obviously, in one sense, he *is* right, because some children are being taught to think in some schools, as long as we agree it is possible to teach someone to think at all. But just as obviously, he is wrong, because some children are not being taught to think in schools, and he is one of them. What I need to do is find some way to get him to remember what school has in fact been like for him. I do not know what his experience has been and so I cannot tell him "what I want." But if he really does reflect about his experience, he probably will begin to see that "children are being taught to think in schools today" is a silly thing to say, not because it is or is not true, but because it is hopelessly inadequate as a statement about what he knows.

Because he knows better than to talk that way. He may continue to say such things, and he may continue to think I am being a bully, a cynic, or a brainwasher when I object. But he knows better.

Which brings us to two fallacies. These are offered here as summaries of the argument to this point.

[48]

Students have strange ways of praising teachers sometimes, as in the following familiar compliment: "He lets you say what you want as long as you back it up with examples and good reasoning." The idea is perfectly sound, of course: students should be allowed to have their own opinions and to learn to think for themselves. A more hallowed piety does not exist in our educational system. But the usual result is the kind of paper, examples of which we have been examining, in which the student says, in effect, "Here is what I think, here are my examples; now get off my back." A teacher who does, at that point, leave the student alone with some comment as "A vigorous argument nicely conducted" earns the standard praise: "He lets you say what you want as long as you back it up."

But the fallacy here lies in the assumption that when we speak or write all we need is an arguable proposition. In fact, of course, anything is arguable, and most broad assertions are demonstrable as well. Thus it is not a sign of liberality or broad-mindedness when a teacher lets a student say anything he likes as long as he backs it up; it is only a sign of weariness. If the teacher objects, some students will feel their right to freedom of speech is being threatened: "Everyone is entitled to his own opinion, and this is what I think." He is not, the student quickly adds, trying to prove that all blacks are apes or that the President should be lynched. Not at all. He is only trying to say that children in schools are being taught to think, and here is the evidence. His attitude is entirely negative, not in the sense of being nay-saying, but in the simple sense that it seeks nothing beyond release from one more assignment.

The fallacy, then, is that a proposition, simply because it is arguable, is therefore worth arguing. As we have seen, the propositions argued in the papers above are all arguable, but all silly too, at best the sport of apprentice debaters, to whom the proper reply is not "Is what you say true?" but "Why do you want to talk that way?" No one seeks to question another's moral and legal right to say silly things, but teachers should ask students why they want to do so.

Perhaps the point can be made more strongly if I introduce the other fallacy here.

The Fallacy of Subjective and Objective

When a teacher asks a student, "Is that what you *want* to say," he implies that the student not only has wants but that he should consult them before he writes. To some, perhaps many, this smacks of something they call "being subjective," and implies that students are only creatures of whim and caprice who should say anything they want to without regard for something usually called "the objective evidence." People say very strange things when they start talking about things being subjective and objective.

This is not the place to enter into the many philosophical problems that can be raised when the discussion turns to the nature of reality; the point I seek to make is not a philosophical but a practical one about writing. We can turn to any arguable proposition. For variety, let us make up a new one: people who perform acts of civil disobedience do great harm to their own cause. This is certainly an arguable proposition; in fact, it can safely be asserted that the statement is true, objectively true. It can be asserted with equal confidence that the statement is false, objectively false. I use the word "objectively" as it is usually used, to mean what it usually means: something is objectively true if it is arguable so as to achieve momentary assent from an unbiased and reasonable listener. If you argue a case, and I consider only your argument and find it reasonable or persuasive, I can say you have stated your case objectively. If you argue a case, and I consider only your argument and find it mad or obscure or meaningless, I can say you have stated your case subjectively. The implication is that we should always seek to be objective. But suppose you argue objectively that people who perform acts of civil disobedience harm their own cause, and it seems to me only one of a great many objective arguments one might make, no better and no worse. Suddenly, I don't care very much whether or not you have been objective, whether your proposition is arguable. If you

[50]

are really trying to persuade me, there is no point in asking myself if you have been objective. Rather, I should ask if what you say is true to experience as I know it. Teachers aren't, or shouldn't be, in the business of being persuaded or dissuaded, and so they should turn the question around and ask, "Does that seem to you true to your experience? Is that all that is true? Have you said best what you think is really the case? Is that what you *want* to say?"

These questions neither assert nor imply that students or anyone else should say whatever pops into his head just to prove he can do it. The questions assume that people have experiences and out of them should draw their material for what they speak, think, and write. Most people do not think the oceans are made of milk, or that all men are wicked and should be destroyed. Nor do they think that "those who civilly disobey greatly harm their own cause" is their best and final utterance on civil turmoil. For all I know, it is demonstrable objectively that all men *should* be destroyed because they *are* completely wicked; rather intelligent people have tried to argue that case. But I do not believe it for a minute, any more than I believe that people are completely good, and these beliefs of mine are not mere subjective opinions either. They are what I know, and if asked to say more, I will not try to prove some arguable proposition.

I will, instead, try to tell you how I look at that aspect of life. And then maybe you will listen. And then we will talk and probably disagree. Because you are you, your experience will have been different from mine. Your experience tells you, perhaps, that all men seek images of their mothers when they choose their wives; mine tells me this is far from being always so. So we will go on talking. Not "objectively" or "subjectively," just talking. I will try to speak clearly and well so you will see what I see, if only for as long as I am speaking. Maybe I will change your mind some, maybe not, and maybe discussion will seem fruitless. But life is like that. It is people trying to say what they most want to say, discovering that proving objectively some arguable proposition is very easy when compared to struggling to say exactly what they believe is true.

The moment of that discovery is a key moment in the career of any writer. It comes when he no longer treats writing, even writing English papers, as a means of getting the world off his back, and when he sees that in his writing he might just be able to say, to himself and to the world, what he most wants to say. After that, perhaps for a long while, words come less easily. But the first big step has been taken, and even if the writer never becomes a good writer or even the writer he had hoped to be, he knows that, whatever else, writing is a form of being himself.

Autobiographical Sketch

Though I am sure that for some I have talked about myself far too much already, for more than is seemly or necessary in a book about writing, I would like now to plunge more openly into a tale of myself and my career as a student forced to write. I do this, not because I think my experience is like everyone's, though probably many will recognize themselves at one or another point along the way, but because I want to come closer to saying what I mean when I say that writing can't be taught.

Like most people, I began to write thinking it was a teacher's matter and not my own. They knew, and I didn't. I diagrammed sentences, I could say at one point (though I can't any more) what the difference is between a complex and a compound sentence. I was told over and over my writing "had" some quality, which did not include coherence or correctness. In high school I would have worried about these things had I thought it made any earthly difference to anyone, but it was quite clear it did not; my English classes were distinguished from my other classes by being so obviously bad. Somehow I got by, got into a college that prided itself on being so good that everyone who entered there, it was assumed, knew how to write. The college, to be sure, was merely evading the fact that most of the students did not know how to write, but maybe their evasion was not such a bad solution, considering the apparent alternatives. In any event, I was told by anyone who took time to say anything about my writing that I was energetic or perceptive, and that these qualities were apparent even though I "wrote badly." This allowed me to continue to treat the matter of writing well as a teacher's matter, and to avoid and scorn teachers who were known for "counting off" for badly written papers. I have no idea what I thought was good writing during any of this time; I liked conscious stylists like E. B. White and George Orwell and would often praise them to my friends for "writing well," but whatever I could mean by that phrase, I did not let such writers serve as a rebuke to my knotted prose.

Whatever of writing can be taught I was not taught, and, except for my incompetence, I was indistinguishable from everyone else. I "had" something, which some called talent or intelligence or brains or even genius, but I didn't have other things: sense, discipline, control, and the ability to take advice. This made it easy for me to think that I really was all right, and anyone who objected to my writing by saying he could not understand it could be rejected on the grounds that he must be fussy, pedantic, a formalist of the worst sort.

No one, thus, in college or beyond, taught me as I now seek to teach my students. No one told me, for instance, that my energy, in its rough and almost consciously unshapen form, was rather uninteresting. I suppose they did not wish to squash me, and probably the most thoughtful of my teachers decided that he could teach me to write only by making me more competent, and that he could make me more competent only by insisting I write shorter and neater sentences.

It is easy to say someone should have tried to teach me to write, but as I look back on my checkered career as a student in English classes, I now see that it worked out much better for me than it did for many. I ignored people who said I didn't know how to write and went my own way, if way it was. After grade school I was never forced to take drills in "fundamentals," never forced to revise papers, or to learn how to spell "separate." As a result, I still make blunders that English teachers aren't supposed to make—if someone asks me, "Who is going," I might say, "He and I," or I might say, "Him and me," so I usually just point. Whenever I read the phrase "relative pronoun," I always think others were better educated than I (than me? No, I think I know that one) and hope I don't ever have to explain relative pronouns to a student. You may well think it is shocking that a man who professes English composition, a Ph.D. no less, is a baby in some of these essential matters, and I am not proud of my clumsiness or ignorance. But I have learned to live with it and always hope that the next time I learn about "he and I" the knowledge will finally stick.

I sailed through graduate school, learning lots of things but not how to write, and took my first teaching job. One day, perhaps a month after the term began, I was carrying on to a colleague about something, undoubtedly being energetic but not very coherent. Slowly, I felt my listener lose attention, and he began staring out of the window. So I stopped, and he turned, and smiling very nicely said to me, "Why do you talk in that boring way?" I knew the statement was kindly meant, and was not crushed by his apparent rudeness. But I was dazed. I had been called brash and unclear and stubborn and rattle-brained, but no one had ever called me boring. It wasn't said about my writing, but it was the only thing ever said to me that, to my knowledge, taught me something real about my writing. It came, to be sure, at the best possible time, and had someone said that to me earlier, I might just have ignored it. But right then I had learned a lot, read a lot, had a lot of notions that were, in fact, borrowed but which I called my own. What I did not have was a way of speaking, because I had never seen the need for one. But here was someone listening carefully to the rush of half-formed, half-assembled sentences, and he was bored. Nothing I said was really thought out, nothing went with anything else except in simple and derivative ways. Quite simply, I did not know what I meant most of the time I spoke or wrote.

After that, writing got harder and harder. Words came easily but satisfaction did not, and, in a way, has never returned. In the intervening years I have had to write a lot, but I have never regained that innocent pleasure in writing I once had. I fuss my sentences more; I wonder if I have said what I mean, if I am saying obvious things, if this sentence clearly follows the one before it. I have learned whatever I have learned about writing under the constant threat of that dazzling and kindly meant "Why do you talk in that boring way?" If my writing ever gets really clear, and if I ever learn to say just what I mean, it will not be because of what I was taught or what I read about writing, about grammar, about organization, about style. It will be because I want to be interesting and am afraid of being dull, because I cannot rest quietly in thinking that the rush, stutter, and confusion that was my expression should be my way of being me.

The Limits of Teaching

All teaching that sets down principles or rules, all teaching that shows students what they are to do, all teaching that, in effect, prescribes, must have as its first commandment: "Be like me." The teacher is himself a model or a maker of models, and the more the teacher works to become such a model, the more the student is presumed to be unworthy until he becomes like the teacher.

Students, of course, will imitate their teachers, especially if they respect or like them; most people like to imitate the habits or manners of those who seem to do something better or more interestingly than they do. No matter how distinctive I try to make my writing, I know it is shot through with my emulation of writers I most admire—George Eliot here, William Empson there, Henry Fielding down the way—and I can see this just as I can see different strains in other writers. We all learn so much by imitating others that, indeed, there is almost no need for any teacher to seek to have his students imitate him. If they like him, they will do it eagerly. In a classroom, in a small, real way, I must try to represent to my students what I believe to be true and important. If all goes well, it is from me that my students will learn about things they never learned before: facts and ideas, both my own and those of others; ways of thinking about writing, about reading, about living. If I talk well, ask interesting questions, say things they have not heard before, I represent my culture well.

But learning is not, of course, merely a matter of learning about, nor is it simply a process whereby a student becomes assimilated into his culture. It is primarily the action whereby a student learns who he is in relation to something outside himself. He seldom does this self-consciously, as though he could sit down to solve a problem in mathematics or to write a paper about *Hamlet* and say to himself, "This way I will learn about myself in relation to something else." Ideally, we all know, when a student somehow becomes "more himself" in the act of learning, he is learning what is most important. Part of a man's becoming more himself will be his becoming, in his own way, like someone else. After all, this whole chapter, in one sense, is my imitation of the man who asked me, "Why do you talk in that boring way?" That is the explicit question I would ask, though perhaps not quite that bluntly, of the authors of all three papers quoted above, and it is the implicit question I ask of any writing that seems to me mechanical, derivative, boring because at bottom thoughtless, a series of arguable propositions. But my imitation is my own, and the man who asked me why I was boring only began a process of change in me that continued long after I had ceased to imitate him.

This is what we expect learning to be like, really, even though we do not always act as though we did. What teachers can do is to ask questions, to praise and criticize, to offer alternate ways of thinking about things. They get someone started, or help him along, in a process of his making himself be careful about himself and the way he thinks and speaks and writes. Listen to the way students talk about teachers they have had. Lots of teachers are talked about, and colorful or eccentric or distinctive ones have stories told about them. The really good teachers also may have stories told about them, but they produce a different effect, because the teacher has become part of the process of the student's growing.

But no one knows how this happens or what a teacher can do to make it happen. The same teacher will affect two students in the same class in very different ways, and the same teacher and the same student can have very different relationships at different times. The teacher always knows he must be aggressive and forward enough to convince the student there is another mind out there intent upon him, yet quiet and withdrawn enough to give the student thinking room whenever it is needed. But no one really knows how to do this, how to plan a class or a course of classes so that this will happen, even to one student. What can be planned is what the teacher himself thinks, and he can sit down late in the summer and work out a long sequence of "classes" which trace out various lines of thinking he finds interesting or important. But when the first class begins, the teacher's thought is only one ingredient in the making of a class, and he has little control over the other ingredients most of the time. Students know this, of course, but teachers forget it all the time. I sometimes catch myself saying or hear another teacher say, "I want to get them to see . . ." or "When you can make them think that . . . ," as though I or any teacher could "get" or "make" a student think anything. Or really want to.

It is possible to "get" or "make" people do all sorts of things if you use enough pressure and are indifferent to the results. If a teacher thinks that having a student spell "existence" and "independence" correctly is enough to accomplish in a given span of time, he can probably find ways to get or make the student do so. But he both forfeits the chance to be doing something else, and enforces the notion that learning is something that can only take place under pressure or threat. Of course, he may not teach the student even that much, and he may end up feeling that if the student did things just a little more neatly that would be enough. But if he seeks neatness he had better not ask for much of it, because even a careful student will become awkward, stiff, and even careless when he feels under the necessity of being neat. If you "get" a student to do one thing, you probably lose all chance of having him do anything else.

Yes, indeed, the proverb says that the journey of a thousand miles must begin with the first step, but easy is the journey in which you know exactly what the first step is. We are back again at the beginning of the chapter, wondering about writing as a skill and as an art. Skills presumably can be taught, because we know what the first steps are, but probably even that is true only of rather simple skills. Part of writing is skill, craft, mechanical learning, of course, but most of that part is learned by everyone when he first learns to speak. Part is art, whatever that may mean. But if we try to say exactly what part is skill, or how much that counts, then we soon get tangled, because we don't know clearly enough what we mean by "skill" and "art" or which comes first or which is more important. We know in a vague way that certain skills in writing are important for a man to function in many daily activities that keep the world going, and without which things would probably fall apart. We know also that to teach these skills as though they were all a man had to know to be educated is a criminal act, because to be educated is not simply to be able to function.

Writing cannot be taught, because it is not a teachable series of actions or patterns; it is the sketching in we do that, for a moment, tells the world and ourselves who we are. The student who begins to see the real limits that his teacher has, no matter how good or bad that teacher be, can also begin to see what he might then do on his own. It would be nice to think we could talk about writing without talking about being a teacher and being a student, but, in fact, most writing in America today is "taught" writing, in classes, with teachers. Given that, it seems that the best thing to do about "getting" or "making" the writing better is to ask about the relationship between teacher and student, and to insist that most of the writing that is done is bad because the relationship is mechanical or unreal to the student. When that relationship is one of power and acceptance of power, writing can be taught that is, at best, no better than the writing machines can do. When that relationship is one of real question, real answer, and real possibility, writing cannot be taught at all. But it can be learned.

3

ORGANIZATION: THE SENSE THAT WRITING MAKES

In this chapter I am going to talk about a variety of things that generally fall under the heading of "Organization," matters we think of as lying somewhere below a writer's ideas and above his grammar and use of particular words. These distinctions are phony, of course, because they imply that one can discuss ideas without discussing the grammar or organization which expresses them, or that one would want to do this if it were possible, and I make the distinctions here only to show later some of the ways all are related one to another. Perhaps I can better describe the subjects I want to discuss in this chapter by saying they are more specific and detailed than those handled in the previous chapter but generally less so than those in Chapter 4.

Relating Two or More Things: The Building of Paragraphs

"Things" is a very loose term here, used to avoid "ideas" on the one hand and "sentences" on the other. Ideas are related to each other by sentences, and sentences are related by ideas, and "related" covers all manner of connection and disconnection.

Although no one knows all the ways one thing can be made to follow another, we all have a sense of sequence, or consecutiveness, which allows us to relax when something we read "makes sense" and to become distracted or upset when something does not. We have lots of words for ways things can be related: logically, naturally, narratively, contrastingly, and so forth, and various writers on language have tried to describe or define what a "logical" connection between two things is, or what strategies are available to writers to make it seem that they have proven a point or made a position effective. In order to avoid making distinctions between logic, rhetoric, exposition, narrative, and the like, I am going to continue to use "relating" as a catch-all term, and this perhaps will allow us to get down to examples of various kinds of relating without further introduction.

The first few examples are all from papers written in answer to the question: "Is it good to change one's mind?"

Order and stability must prevail in order to have any form of organized civilization. However, this does not mean that man cannot change his mind on any subject. We are the products of the thinking of our environment and, therefore, hold many preconceived ideas on subjects that we have not fully encountered ourselves. For example, I have some ideas on love, sex, and marriage which can only be proved personally. Some of my ideas will not be changed, because I will not have to apply them to my own life. However, my mind must be open to change in my daily affairs if reason proves another idea to be better, but some of my basic ideas will remain unchanged. I believe in representative democracy with much basic stability, but it must also have a reasonable amount of flexibility to adapt to new situations and ideas. I do not intend to alter this opinion in my later life. I also consider my religion to be fixed in my mind. I may add new ideas or modify my present opinions, but I will not change from my basic Protestant belief in God. I also hold the conviction that freedom with orderliness is the best form of civilization for man. My belief in freedom and the dignity of the human being will not change. My belief in the necessity of the search for truth will also remain constant.

One way of questioning the writer of this paper is to ask how the words used to do the relating of two things—"however," "therefore," and "because" in this instance—have really made clear the relationship. "He was tall. However, he had blue eyes." Clearly, the "however" there is nonsense, and it is easy to see how nonsense or coherence is the result of careless or careful use of "moreover," "nevertheless," "but," "and," "therefore," "thus," "so," "now," "since," and all the hundreds of words we use to make relations. Think what one can do with a word like "luckily," and how many different relations can be established simply by moving the word "only" around to different parts of a sentence.

We will look at some of these possible combinations later on. First, though, let's examine the paragraph quoted above and the various relations it makes. An outline of the paragraph looks like this:

Statement and counterstatement

    1. Order and stability must prevail . . . (1st sentence)
    2. However, this does not mean . . . (2nd sentence)

Amplification and support

    1a. We are the products . . . (3rd, 4th, and 5th sentences)
    2a. However, my mind must be open to change . . . (6th sentence, opening)
    1a. . . . but some of my basic ideas will not change (6th sentence, completion; 7th sentence, opening)
    2a. . . . but it must also . . . (7th sentence, ending)

Resolution: I do not intend to alter this opinion . . . (8th sentence)

Restatement of 1. and 2. with new examples:

    1b. I also consider my religion . . . (9th sentence)
    2b. I may add . . . (10th sentence, opening)
    1a. . . . but I will not change . . . (10th sentence, ending, to end of paragraph)

In one sense, the pattern is very neat. The writer sees a need both for firm opinions and for flexibility (as who does not?).

He proceeds to weave statement and counterstatement through-out the paragraph, as he considers his beliefs about private matters, like love and religion, and public matters, like government. The weaving is done in such a way that what is obviously a private matter (love and sex) is followed by what is obviously a public matter (government), and public and private are blended in his final sentences (freedom, the dignity of human-ity, the search for truth). All the sentences are complete, and the sense of orderliness is maintained throughout.

Yet, the paragraph seems to me either hurried and thoughtless, or else intellectually bankrupt. The key word is the "however" in the second sentence, because its usage shows that, instead of maintaining complexity, the author is vacillating, weaving as a football player does in a desire to avoid being tackled, rather than weaving as a rug-maker does in his desire to blend and reconcile different colors and patterns. The first two sentences are:

> Order and stability must prevail in order to have any form of organized civilization. However, this does not mean that man cannot change his mind on any subject.

If you take that first sentence by itself, and add "however" as a beginning for a second sentence, you can think of quite a few sentences that could follow:

> However, a little anarchy always helps a civilization stay civilized.

> However, violence is unavoidable, and attempts to abolish violence can only be more violent and bloody than that whose end is sought.

> However, no order is worth preserving that does not acknowledge and uphold the lurching and fickle way people naturally lead their lives.

One could go on. But "however" means a turn, a contradiction, an antithesis, none of which are offered by the second sentence as written: "However, this does not mean that man cannot change his mind on any subject." To which the best reply is, "Whoever thought it did?" There should be no "however" here, for "order" and "change of mind" are relatable by "however" only if "order" means something close to total silence and "change of mind" means sudden and violent shifts in thinking. It is not very likely that the writer intends either of these meanings, and the bland tone of both sentences and those that follow shows that he is not interested in making special definitions for his main terms.

In fact, the moment the absurdity of this "however" is clear, the rest of the paragraph falls to pieces, and the repetition of the absurdity in more obvious form in the sixth sentence, "However, my mind must be open to change . . . but some of my basic ideas will remain unchanged," only compounds the absurdity and cannot organize the paragraph. The tenth sentence pulls the same trick, "I may add or modify, but I will not change," so as to render the words almost totally meaningless. Suddenly, it becomes possible to see other places in the paragraph where very strange things are taking place. Look first at the "therefore" in the third sentence: "We are the products of the thinking of our environment, and, therefore, hold many preconceived ideas . . ." This is no disaster, and a rewriting of the opening clause seems to justify the "therefore": "We learn to accept many things unquestioningly . . ." But the moment the "therefore" is straightened out that way, the two parts of the sentence repeat each other: we are given preconceived ideas and therefore we have them. The whole enterprise is sufficiently in trouble to warrant complete revision, and the moment one sees this, one sees the sentence can be taken out entirely without losing a thing.

Now look at the "because" in the fifth sentence: "Some of my ideas will not be changed because I will not have to apply them to my own life." This is a non sequitur, one that is interesting because it raises such questions as: "How does one change his ideas?" and "In what sense does anyone ever apply ideas to life?" The problems are complex enough that they are not going to be solved in a sentence, and no revision will make the "because" work. Perhaps, if he could see this, the author might then begin to see that he has not really asked himself what happens to him as his experience encounters his preconceived ideas.

There are many ways to question a paragraph like this one, but most teachers will be so struck by its fatuousness, and a few will be so pleased by its apparent coherence that they will start accusing or applauding very quickly. To ask about the way it relates its parts, though, seems to me much more likely to elicit that bewilderment one wants from such a student. Look at the leaky "with" in "I believe in representative democracy with much basic stability . . ." It would be hard to show this writer what is wrong with his "with," and easier to engage him with his "however," "because," "therefore," and "but." The "with," though, is telltale, because it simply evades the question the whole paragraph evades concerning the relation between the individual's mind and the need for social order. The "with" evades by not asking what the relationship between democracy and stability is or should be; only "and" could say as little. If, just once, the writer could see the intellectual failure expressed in his "with," he might then begin to see how many ways there are of relating things, how interesting the questions can become when he asks if he wants a "for" or a "moreover" at a given point.

Here is a second paragraph on changing one's mind:

I cannot constantly change my mind, moving from one position to another on mere whim or snap judgment. I must change my mind only after considering the whole instead of the parts. For example, last year in American history, I read the Amherst booklet, *American Revolution: Economic or Political?* The first article (of about eight) was Beard's economic interpretation. It convinced me, and I changed my mind from the childish "No taxation without representation" slogan theories. The next historian tore the first essay to pieces, arguing that the cause was political. Again I was convinced, for the latter presented all the counter-arguments to the first essay, and then presented its own viewpoint. The third blasted both apart, arguing that the cause was a combination of the two factors. This I thought was the most cogent of all. In short, each historian had convinced me of the rightness of his explanation. Upon finishing the booklet, I thought of how my mind had fluctuated, and discovered that hasty changes of opinions based on a limited number of facts are rash. I could not form a thorough interpretation of the American Revolution until I had considered a wealth of answers and facts. I did not have a complete picture by any means, yet I was considering an imperfect whole as well as isolated parts.

What is remarkable about this paragraph is certainly not its neat, straightforward organization, or its depth of insight into a problem. The example it offers is a real example, unlike the examples offered in the first paper, which are no more than subjects named. The interesting thing is the way the example seems to reform the writer's thinking and writing from simple and even idle assertions to a conclusion that begins to make more complicated relationships. The first sentence, "I cannot constantly change my mind, moving from one position to another on mere whim or snap judgment" is defective in many ways, and changing "moving" to a neater "by moving" or "or move" is not going to help much. In the second sentence, the defects lie within the province of the connecting and relating words: "I must change my mind only after considering the whole instead of the parts." The writer presumably does not mean that he *must* change his mind even after considering the whole problem; he means he must change his mind, if at all, after considering the whole problem. The "must" can stay if the "only" goes, and probably it is the "must" that should go, to be replaced by "should." The "instead of" here is standard usage, but slipshod too, because the writer does not mean that he will not consider the parts at all, but that he will consider them as they relate one to another to make a whole. His example, by the way, offers one of those rare instances where it can be legitimately claimed that there is a whole for the person to consider; most human affairs, as we all know, must be conducted without our knowing if what we are considering is really a whole. It certainly is to be hoped that the writer has not been misled into thinking that the eight essays in his booklet represent the whole of human thinking about the economic and political forces at work in the American Revolution.

But that is, at the moment, by the way. After his flat and

thoughtless start, the writer offers his example, and afterward shows that he sees complications of which the opening sentences are ignorant: "I did not have a complete picture by any means, yet I was considering an imperfect whole as well as isolated parts." This is, in one sense, only a rewriting of the second sentence of the paragraph, but in place of the mechanical relationship of "must" to "only," he offers his "yet" to show that, though he had little, he had more than at first. Furthermore, the "yet" makes the relationship between "complete" and "imperfect" precise. There is a real and modest sense of triumph implied by that "yet," and the "as well as" is a vast improvement on the earlier "instead of," because it shows that the whole he considers is made of parts and not of some mysterious and wonderful wholeness. This last sentence is nothing great, but the relationships it makes are clear and sensible, because the "yet" is right, as the "only" in the second sentence and the "discovered" and the "until" in those just preceding are not.

We might ask, for a moment, what would happen to that last sentence if the writer had used "because" instead of "yet," thereby making it read: "I did not have a complete picture by any means, because I was considering an imperfect whole as well as isolated parts." This too makes sense, but of a quite different kind, for the sense of triumph is lost, and the "as well as" is now no longer neat. The moment one can say that, one is also saying that the sentence as written has a kind of coherence which no other in the first two examples has; if the relating words do organize the thought of the sentence so that a change in them would force a change in other words, then thought is taking place.

Now a last example:

I do not like to change my mind or admit that it has been changed. In fact I seldom am willing to tell anyone that I have ever changed my mind about anything. When I get into an argument and I care about the subject and think I know something about it, and it turns out that the person I am talking to is more persuasive than I, I don't tell him so unless he insists or I am really excited by the new thoughts he has given me. I remember once arguing with my father, who was for Nixon, and I was for John F. Kennedy. He did not try to contradict what I

[66]

said in praise of Kennedy, but kept asking me how much of the country Kennedy would be able to govern. The anti-Eastern and anti-Catholic feeling in the country is so strong, he said, that if Kennedy is elected, most of the country between the Appalachians and the Rockies and south of the Mason-Dixon line would go on fighting him and getting Congress to do nothing. He was giving me a whole new way to think about elections and government. But because I didn't want to tell him this, I kept on attacking Nixon for his conservatism and praising Kennedy for his new ideas, so we ended the discussion without his knowing that I had changed my mind. Because of this conversation I have changed the way I think about politics. But I have kept the way my father and I talk to each other, for that too is important.

This paragraph may not seem quite as neatly organized as the two preceding examples, but if the emphasis in the first sentence, "I do not like to change my mind," is as much on "like" as on "change," then the subject is what the writer likes as well as what he does. This contrast is maintained throughout, and the relating words do a good job of keeping the contrast alive. The first "or" makes a distinction which later is important, between doing something and admitting having done it. The "in fact" is used loosely, because the facts of the issue are not in question, but in fact "in fact" is often used simply for emphasis. The persistent qualifying "and"s in the next sentence do a neat job of paring down the example to the one the writer wants, so that he is not left implying that this particular kind of argument—where he cares, knows something, and is up against a better arguer—is the only kind there is. This kind of sentence is notably missing from the first two paragraphs; they really do hinge broad generalizations on one example, while this writer narrows the generalization down to the point where the example not only illustrates the generalization but is sufficient to demonstrate its validity.

After the example is over, we come back to the original generalization. It would have been easy for the writer to simplify both the example and the conclusion with a "So I learned the advantages of an open mind," or some such. Instead, with his "but because," he keeps the example alive and the generalization more pointed. This "but because" is, then, nicely rounded out with two concluding sentences, one beginning with "because" and the other with "but," so that the example keeps causing the change of mind. The "but" keeps showing the writer's handling of his relationship with his father, and the "because" and the "but" are both real and important for the whole paragraph. There is nothing complicated about this writer's use of his relating words, and, for that matter, there is nothing really complicated about the paragraph, but it is neatly done and is much less mechanical in its handling of the eternal problem of relating example to generalization than are either of the first two.

There are, to repeat, many ways of talking about these paragraphs, and I have emphasized the words that relate and connect, because they offer a way for a writer to think about his own paragraphs, such that he can see if the things that ostensibly are going together really do go together as he wants. It also keeps one from the usual nonsense about the structure of paragraphs: topic sentences, logical succession of ideas, clearly stated conclusions, and the like.

No one knows what should go into a paragraph until he starts to write it and begins to gain a sense of its direction. There are no good rules for starting or ending paragraphs beyond what common sense dictates. Later on in this chapter, I will talk about the ways in which following rules about the organization of a paragraph often leads writers to write consecutive paragraphs that bear no clear relation to each other, each being its own tight little island, entire unto itself, so that the overall organization is sacrificed to isolated set pieces. What is interesting, what can even be quite exciting, is the way, within sentences and within paragraphs, things can become related so that both the writer as he writes and the reader as he reads are constantly aware that new, different, and even important relationships are being established.

This is not a matter about which it is easy to dogmatize; what can be done is to show how really fine writing constantly is establishing these relationships. Many people admit that there is such fine writing in the world, but few would allow that such writing is well within the reach of the average writer in an English or Language Arts course. So, rather than look at a gem from George Orwell or E. B. White, let me quote an excerpt from a freshman asked to name the advantages and disadvantages of rote learning:

> Rote learning is concerned with words, sounds, shapes, but not with the meanings these symbols convey. When I learn by rote I use the meanings of symbols to learn the symbols instead of using the symbols to understand the meanings. Thus, in German, I arrange the prepositions which take the dative in alphabetical order: auf, aus, auser, and so on, and don't ask what the prepositions mean. I take the alphabetical order and build relationships in sound on top of it, so that I remember "nach-von-zu" because the words are arranged alphabetically, and also because I learn that "nach-von-zu" sounds like "knock one shoe." Now I know that this is "wrong," in one sense, because learning the sound "knock one shoe" is not going to help me learn what "nach" means, and I must learn what "nach" means sooner or later. But, in another sense, it is "right," because in my experience rote learning enables you to learn enough so you can begin to feel familiar with whatever is being learned. So I learn "knock one shoe," and it serves as one of my passports to looking at German sentences, and every time I see that little "nach," I know it's not something brand new, I know it is a preposition, and I know the word following is in the dative case. I am beginning to think that, if I could understand what the dative case is, I would then be well on my way to understanding what "nach" means. So I can't find any good way to learn what the dative case is by rote, but if I can find a way I'll use it, because I have so few good ways of learning *any* German, and I take any that come along.

What I like about this paragraph is the way it seems to have been written without the hand of the writer ever leaving the page. There are a lot of rather nice twists and turns in it, and each one is clearly connected to the one preceding. Some of this is done simply by linking many of the sentences with a word at the beginning of one sentence that signifies the relationship of the one before with the one to come: when, thus, now, but, so. It is a simple device, and you will often hear it said that in the best writing such linking words aren't necessary because the links will be conveyed in other ways. It is certainly true that some very good writing, particularly of a kind that uses terse phrases and short sentences, not only does not need but

[69]

would be made awkward by such phrases. But most writing is not like that, and most writers need not feel they demean themselves, hurt their writing, or insult their audience by seeing themselves as guides in need of offering signals. Often there is no other way to indicate what the relationship between two sentences is. Look, for instance, at the "now" with which the writer of the above paper turns his whole paragraph around. He has begun with his definition and his example, not with his thesis, and he has led the example to its conclusion. The effect of the "Now I know that this is 'wrong,' in one sense" is to indicate that the turn is coming, and also to show his reader he is perfectly aware of all the possible arguments against rote learning. Take away the "now," the quotation marks around "wrong," and the "in one sense," and all relations with the preceding sentences and with the reader break down and won't resume until some new relating words are encountered. Try this:

> . . . so that I remember "nach-von-zu" because the words are arranged alphabetically, and also because I learn that "nach-von-zu" sounds like "knock one shoe." This is wrong. Learning the sound "knock one shoe" is not going to help me learn what "nach" means. It is right. In my experience rote learning enables you to feel familiar with what is being learned.

In a sense I have changed nothing, but in another sense I have put my reader into a bed of randomly arranged nails just by getting rid of or slightly altering the relating words. The relation of the wrongness to the rightness has been almost completely destroyed (and in the process "It is right" has become unintelligible), and with that destruction, all that is interesting about the paragraph is blurred or lost.

Relating words, of course, are not confined to the beginning of sentences, and here a good many relating words organize internally. In the revision I wrote above I changed the last sentence from ". . . rote learning enables you to learn enough so you can begin to feel familiar with whatever is being learned" to ". . . rote learning enables you to feel familiar with whatever is being learned." I began my revision by leaving out only the relating words "enough so," and then discovered that left "to learn" and "can begin" with no satisfactory use, and so cut out the whole sequence. There is nothing drastically wrong with the revised version, and some might prefer it simply because it is shorter. But the point has been simplified badly, and in the revision the sense of two different but closely related kinds of learning is lost. That "enough so" maintains the relationship between "knock one shoe" and the whole question of the dative, and thereby keeps the paragraph together.

These must seem like small points, and in a way they are, because this kind of precision usually involves only one or two words. Also, it must be repeated, what is involved here is not writing that seeks to be flashy or impressive, but simply writing that is trying to be clear, plain, and precise. There will be no lightning bursts of metaphoric brilliance or dense pursuit of abstract profundities. Someone is asked a question, and he seeks to give an honest answer. It wasn't his question and probably isn't his subject, but perhaps he sees a way to make his answer his own, an expression of something he knows. What he knows is almost always a matter of the relationships he establishes, between example and generalization, between one part of a narrative and the next, between the idea and the counteridea that the writer sees is also relevant, between his experience and what he knows of the experience of others—in short, between any two parts of his knowledge. On the one hand this, on the other hand that; not this, but that; not just this, but also that; if this, then that; because this, that; that as an example of this; not this until that; yet, moreover, since, so, and: the list is potentially endless, and by inquiring into the exact relationship between things, a writer discovers what he knows, the words he wants.

". . . a writer discovers what he knows, the words he wants." The matter of relating can extend down to the smallest matters and still be interesting. A tiny change, "a writer discovers what he knows, and then the words he wants," changes the relationships between the two clauses. To add "and then" is to say that the act of discovering is distinct from the act of finding the wanted words, as though knowledge preceded language in this instance. But regardless of whether it is ever possible to know something without knowing the words that express the knowledge, here the act of discovering is the act of finding words; for the writer there is no other way. To add "and then," in this case, would be to blur the sense of the entire preceding paragraph, and even to add "and" is to imply, however faintly, that the clauses describe separate actions. It is very important in this sentence that there be no relating words, because "what he knows" and "the words he wants" can only be properly related by modifying "discovers" equally and simultaneously. Relating words would only make the activities have some other relationship to each other than that of simultaneous action.

In this example a comma is the right relating "word." In others the semicolon can help because it can create a close but not quite clear relationship between two sentences. I confess I see little other use for the semicolon, and writers who use a great many semicolons usually are not asking themselves how they want to relate their sentences. Some writers try never to use semicolons, but this ignores their real, if limited, use. Here are two examples:

> Minorities at various extremes always think the middle ways occupied by the majority are bland; the majority always thinks the minorities are dangerous.

> A great writer, and Shakespeare is of course a great writer, is not someone who can be understood by means of logic; he needs readers of sympathy and imagination.

The semicolon is "correct" enough in both sentences, but I think it is better in the second than in the first. The first can easily be made into one sentence by changing the semicolon to a comma or by adding a simple connective like "and," "while," or "but," depending on the writer's intention. It can also easily be made into two sentences, because what are now separated by the semicolon are really equal and in balance. In the second sentence above, however, the clause after the semicolon is clearly subsequent to and dependent on what precedes it. To change the semicolon to a comma is to make an awkward comma splice, and to change the semicolon to a period is to make the two parts more independent than they really are. As it is, with the semicolon, the sentence stops for a moment and leans on the semicolon, so that when it continues, it offers a sense of released energy which finishes the sentence with emphasis. Of course, the sentence could be simplified and rewritten to avoid the semicolon: "A great writer like Shakespeare must be read with sympathy and imagination and not with logic." But the revision cannot obtain the same effect of one or more clauses building to a momentary pause and then being released into an emphatic conclusion, so that the semicolon, in effect, creates a relation between the clauses.

We are about to move onto what may seem trivial—the potential uses of "and" and "but." So let me say again that, of all the ways there are of talking and thinking about organization in composition, those concerned with apparently small matters, like the relation of clause to clause and sentence to sentence, are, in fact, the most important for any writer. The reason is simple: anyone who gets in the habit of asking himself how he really wants to relate two words, phrases, clauses, and sentences will find himself inevitably asking how to build groups of sentences into paragraphs and paragraphs into whole papers. Inevitably. But if you start thinking about organization as a matter that requires outlining and a large framework before beginning, you may end up with a wonderful paper, or you may end up with a paper that bears the same relation to its ideal fulfillment as a cartoon drawing does to a man. The life of any writer is expressed in his sense of small, moment-to-moment relationships, nerve, sinew, muscle. It is easy to learn to make outlines, but much harder and more interesting to learn to write with the mind never leaving the page.

Potential Uses of "And" and "But"

Perhaps the easiest way to show what can be done with "and" and "but" is to give some examples in which these words can alter the context of the whole sentence:

Denmark, Sweden, and Norway joined the majority in the vote. [The Scandinavian countries showed solidarity.]

Denmark, Sweden, Norway, but not Finland, joined the majority . . . [Though there were reasons for Scandinavian solidarity, the Finns had other, stronger reasons. Perhaps the Russians . . .]

Denmark, Sweden, Norway, and not Finland . . . [Here there are no reasons to expect the Finns to join the others, and considerations are not geographic, but political, economic, ideological.]

Denmark, Sweden, Norway, and Portugal . . . [The cold war is on, and Western allies and Western neutrals unsurprisingly join together.]

Finland and Iceland voted with the minority, but Denmark, Sweden, and Norway . . . [Interesting; are new power blocs being formed near the Arctic Circle?]

Finland and Iceland voted with the minority, and Denmark, Sweden, and Norway . . . [This blandest of sentences is perhaps the most suggestive of all. It may be the writer finds the world unintelligible but is not surprised—thus the telltale "and"; it may be that the writer has some inside information and reveals it by not acting surprised at what outsiders might consider surprising.]

These are simple sentences, too, the sort one could expect to find in a straightforward news report, but they show the kind of nuance or emphasis that can be gotten into flat sentences with a switch of an "and" or a "but."

Something a little more complicated can be seen when we look at "and" and "but" at the beginning of sentences. I can remember being told on and off in school, usually by people who didn't seem much interested in writing, never to begin a sentence with "and" and seldom to begin one with "but" or one of its synonyms like "however" or "nevertheless." The reason behind such prohibitions is clear enough: "and" and "but" are meant to be conjunctions within sentences and not between sentences. Clearly, one does not want "Denmark, Sweden, and Norway voted for the motion. And Finland too," or "I will wait for you. But only until 5 o'clock." There is a kind of mind—I will call it a "what if" mind—that has little use for either "and" or "but" at the beginning of a sentence. The mind that asks, "What if . . ." usually likes to see sentences move straightforwardly:

> If the city does not develop a rapid transit system, an inevitable sequence follows. Within five years the highways now in existence will have become intolerably crowded at peak hours. Great demand will have been created for more freeways that cut up more and more of the central city and extend further and further into the countryside. There will be so little land left downtown that its price will rise enormously, small businesses operating in old buildings will gradually be forced out, and the area will be rebuilt to accommodate developers who can invest millions of dollars in skyscrapers. Out in the country land prices will soar, cheap housing tracts will appear, and another large tract of forest and farm land will be destroyed.

At its best, this kind of writing can be rather impressive. No relating words here, just one "if" and a host of implied "then"s. It is the secret of most good storytelling. What if a young man, call him Huck, ran away from his Aunt Polly? What if George Wallace were elected President of the United States? What if you woke one Tuesday morning and wished it were Saturday, and found out it suddenly *was* Saturday? What if . . . , then, then, then. The "what if" world at its best is the world of enchanted things, because a great writer who asks what if something happened knows that this, this, this will follow. As night follows day, he will tell you, if the rapid transit system vote fails, these are the consequences.

Most of us most of the time are not quite this sure of ourselves. We think that if the rapid transit vote fails, this will happen, but that will happen, too. We are unable to lay down our sentences like planks, one after the other, bang, bang, bang, because, very often, to write that way is to simplify ourselves into arguable propositions. One of the most obvious signs of a thoughtful person is his sense of "but," and one of the easiest ways for a writer to avoid simplification is to ask himself if his sentences, each one of them, should begin with an "and" or a "but," implied or real.

Here is a paragraph, taken sentence by sentence, written by

someone asked to describe the relationship between his principles and his education:

> There is a great portion of my life which education does not seem to touch.

At this point, the writer wants to add that there is *also* a great portion of his life that is not touched by any of his statable principles. The implied connection is "and":

> And I am beginning to believe that much of my life does not touch my listed noble principles.

Very good. In two sentences, three areas are neatly related to each other: life, education, principles. At this point, he wants to insist that, despite their isolation from his life and education, his principles are real:

> I do have these principles, they do matter to me, but so often they don't seem connected with anything I am doing.

There is a "but" here, but the connection between this sentence and the one preceding is strictly "and," so much so that the writer might well have seen that the second and third sentences repeat so much that he did not need two sentences at all.

At this point, the writer tries this:

> A saint will find a way to serve the Lord in all he does—I am no saint.

It is clear in which direction he *wants* to go: the unreality of his principles is not going to bother him, because such unreality is normal. But he has, I think, gotten a little combative with his reader. Having written that his principles don't seem to be connected with what he is doing, he seems to think that fact needs a defense, so he writes an implied "but." Better, I think, would have been an implied "and" and an example of the way his life leaves him disconnected from his principles. There is no need to be defensive, and there is need to show more clearly this "life" he speaks of.

[76]

Once having become defensive, he seems to lose track of himself:

> A saint will find a way to serve the Lord in all he does—I am no saint. Education will affect me and many of my lesser principles—principles on seeing truth, penmanship, and sleep have been radically altered since I came to college.

The relation implied between the two sentences is a strong "and." But when he says, "Education will affect me," he is contradicting his opening sentence, and when he adds "my lesser principles" he is weaseling, because he wants to imply but not state that somehow his education is attacking him but will not get at his greater principles. If this is so, if his education is attacking him, then he should revamp the whole paragraph; as it is, he falls into a kind of heavy humor. His "principles" about penmanship and sleep are, of course, not part of his education at all, and his principle about seeing truth almost certainly is not, or should not be, a "lesser principle" at all. Having plunged this far, he can only finish up with more "and" writing and hope his paragraph comes out somewhere:

> These are the principles education usually touches; only rarely does formal, scholastic education ever seem to come close to my most important principles.

This follows from the preceding sentence, just as that followed from the one before it, but we can show the simplification that has taken place by comparing this with the second sentence: "And I am beginning to believe that much of my life does not touch my listed noble principles." The most interesting relationship made in the paragraph comes with that "and" and its establishment of the three discrete areas: life, education, principles. After this, the "life" is lost, first in the semiredundancy of the third sentence, then in the apologetic fourth sentence, after which only education and principles are left in a shadowy confrontation.

A thorough rewriting of the paragraph is not needed here, but a redirecting of its opening sentences can show at least one way it could have gone:

There is a great portion of my life which education does not seem to touch. And I am beginning to believe that much of my life is lived independently of my principles, too. I learn in history class about the rascals and the egotists who founded many of the Protestant sects. And I "believe in" my Protestant faith. But neither what I learn nor what I believe in really has much to do with my daily conduct of my relationships with the teachers and other students around me.

Neither of the "and"s which begin sentences in the above example are strictly necessary, but both keep the traffic moving rightly; the "but" at the beginning of the last sentence does seem to me necessary. Regardless of whether "and" or "but" are in fact there, however, a sense of their potentially being there at the beginning of all the sentences does a great deal to give the writer a chance to ask himself what his bearings are, and where, moment-to-moment and sentence-to-sentence, he is going.

Let me add here some remarks about more fancy uses of "and" and "but." There is a kind of story almost everyone has read an example of once. It isn't long, and when you sit down to read, it looks as if it should go rather quickly. But it turns out, perhaps because the writing is very lush or the pace is very slow or all the speakers are long-winded, that, short as it is, the story is hard to get through. How to describe such a story: short *but* interminable. Suppose, however, you want to stigmatize it even more. Try: short *and* interminable. To say the story is short but interminable is to state a paradox; to say it is short and interminable is to imply that we should not expect such a story to be anything except interminable. If I write novels that are short and interminable, it is then clear that I am so bad that it is no paradox and no surprise that my work is impossible to finish, no matter how short it is.

It is a rather neat sort of trick. A golf course that is long but easy is one not laden with traps and narrow fairways; a course that is long and easy is flat, empty, baked hard. A girl who is pretty but repulsive is a tease or has bad breath; a girl who is pretty and repulsive has automatic good looks, perhaps, or is responsible more to Revlon than to God for her prettiness. A teacher who is tough but fair is a highly principled bear; a teacher who is tough and fair shows that the only way to be fair is simultaneously to be tough.

"Logic" as a Means of Creating
Slackness. And "Related"
Paragraphs That Don't Relate.

People teach "outlining." Once upon a time I tried to do it myself. In many courses in composition and in many books about writing, "logic" is taught or at least glanced at. I used to try to do that, too. At the time I usually concluded that I wasn't doing the job properly, because my students seemed to write as loosely and disconnectedly as ever. Only later did I begin to realize that perhaps what my students were doing to make their papers loose and unconnected was outlining them and filling them in with "logic."

The usual way to begin discussion of organization in writing is with larger units, "outlining." But I began where I did because I believe that the real acts of organizing and achieving form are the little ones, the sentence-by-sentence ones. If the writer can relate clearly and exactly, in countless little ways, then almost inevitably the larger-scale organizations, the shapes of the whole, will take care of themselves. There are some writers who can write gorgeous sentences and cogent paragraphs but who cannot build sound wholes. But not many. Much more common are writers who can offer shells without innards, outlines that outline but say little or nothing.

For instance, here is a complete paper written on the subject of Hamlet as a tragic hero:

> Hamlet has, for more than three hundred years, been a puzzle to audiences and readers. To some, "the melancholy Dane" is neurotic, to others he is wise; some point to his weakness, others to his strength. A few go so far as to deny Hamlet the title of "tragic hero." Although I cannot hope to say anything original about this play, I can isolate certain aspects of Hamlet's role as tragic hero: his courage, his honesty, and his deep feelings. These

traits, when combined, give Hamlet the stature that a tragic hero must have.

Although Hamlet does a great deal of talking, one of his outstanding traits is his courage. Ophelia speaks of him as a soldier. He dares to follow the Ghost, even though Horatio and the other characters warn it may be dangerous. After the play-within-a-play, Hamlet lives in a constant state of danger, but not once does he say he is afraid or allow the fact he is in danger deter him from doing what he knows he must do. At the end, he bravely walks into the duel with Laertes, even though he agrees with Horatio beforehand that he may be walking into a trap. At every point in the play where courage is called for, Hamlet shows he has this trait.

Hamlet's honesty consists of his doing what he believes is right, even though this means cutting himself off from everyone. Claudius, Hamlet's mother, and the others of the new court are kind and polite to Hamlet at the beginning, but Hamlet rejects them because he senses their falseness. Twice he disregards Horatio's advice when he is physically threatened, and he constantly shuns the advice of anyone who asks him to compromise his integrity and to go along with Claudius, Rosencrantz, Guildenstern, Laertes, and others he suspects are false. Things would have been simpler had he forgotten the Ghost, but that he could not and would not do. It would have been easier to invite the players to perform a nondescript play, but Hamlet risks everything because he thinks he must.

Last but not least, life affects Hamlet more deeply than anyone else. Other heroes are brave and have integrity, but few ask so much of life and feel so strongly about it. For Hamlet, what is at stake is not his mother's frailty but the frailty of women, and deep reflection leads him to question whether men should live at all. When Horatio warns him against fighting Laertes, Hamlet says: "We defy augury. There's divinity in the fall of the sparrow." He is never a victim of the circumstances of his particular life; instead, he takes those particulars and uses them as material for profound speculation about all of life. In this way, Hamlet's situation achieves the degree of universality it needs in order for Hamlet to emerge as a tragic hero.

Courage, honesty, deep feeling—these certainly do not exhaust Hamlet's characteristics. But they do begin to show why Hamlet is important, why he cannot accept the world he lives in, why he is a true tragic hero.

[80]

This is not a very good paper, but it is not unlike lots of papers that are written, and its faults cannot easily be isolated by someone interested in laying down forms and outlines for writing papers. It describes, in order, three traits of Hamlet's that contribute to his heroism, and it surrounds its three central paragraphs with an introduction and a conclusion. Isn't that the way it is done, teacher? No, that is not the way it is done.

The three paragraphs collectively commit one crime, and individually commit another. The collective assumption is that "Hamlet as tragic hero" is best described as a series of characteristics, none of which has much to do with any of the others or with anything else about Hamlet. Thus we have three piles, marked in turn "Courage," "Honesty" and "Deep feeling," and onto each pile is thrown whatever is reasonably allowable as an example of each trait. By making the piles, the writer implies that Hamlet's courage is separate from his honesty, and that neither has anything to do with his deep feeling. The paragraphs serve as isolation wards, and the "structure" of the whole allows the writer to avoid asking how these separate characteristics are related to each other or the play as a whole. In simple truth, that which *can* be easily divided into separate compartments *should* not, therefore, thus be divided.

Hamlet, like most characters and all people, is not simply a series of traits. We often find it convenient to speak of Hamlet's courage or Einstein's genius or Lincoln's wit, and thereby to isolate a person's particular strength or weakness. But we know that no one is simply the sum or a simple combination of the traits that can be isolated from him. If we want to identify a single characteristic, we are doing the identifying, the isolating, the separating, and in the person such isolation does not exist. Hamlet is indeed at times courageous, and he has integrity and deep feelings, and these qualities do contribute to his moral stature, but to isolate each from the others and all three from Hamlet as a whole is to distort the character and the play for the sake of the outline of our argument about him.

So, too, with the handling of each particular trait. Having decided he needs to identify those actions of Hamlet's that show courage, the writer then makes the same kind of distortion. He takes an event, Hamlet's going to see the Ghost in Act I, and he says it is an example of courage. That is certainly a demonstrable proposition. The Ghost appears and beckons to Hamlet, and obviously will not speak unless Hamlet leaves his friends and goes with the Ghost alone. It is arguable that to do this requires courage. It is also arguable that to do this requires intelligence, love of father, and curiosity. But just as the character is distorted by the writer's isolating individual traits that can be listed, so, too, is the incident distorted by its being made an example of only one of these traits. The lists this writer offers within his paragraphs are like his big list of three major traits: they isolate, they distort by isolating, they keep things unrelated. For instance: "Ophelia speaks of him as a soldier. He dares to follow the Ghost even though Horatio and the other characters warn it may be dangerous." Those sentences go together only in the sense that both list items which the writer feels he can safely put into his pile marked "Courage." Ophelia does indeed speak of Hamlet as a soldier, but that by itself indicates little, as she does so at a moment when nostalgically she speaks of all his virtues: "O what a noble mind is here o'er thrown: The courtier's, soldier's, scholar's eye, tongue, sword." Of course this is "evidence" that Hamlet is a soldier, but of course also, that is not Ophelia's (or Shakespeare's) point about him here. In any event, the fact that Ophelia calls him a soldier and that two acts earlier he broke away from Horatio to join the Ghost are not really related. Hamlet is not a coward—no one ever thought he was. But that is to say very little about him, just as to say that Ophelia calls him a soldier is to say very little about the speech in which she says this. In extracting traits, in making lists of places where these traits can be said to be displayed, the play and the character of the hero become quarries from which lists can be taken, instead of being things to be looked at, pondered, explored.

The point can be summarized this way: if, in order to achieve form for the paper, a writer must ignore or distort the form of what he is talking about, the paper is doing the writer and his subject a disservice. The tendency to make lists, both within paragraphs and out of separate paragraphs, can be really damaging in this regard. The list is the easiest kind of organization, and, in some instances, it is also the best. But items in a list numbered one, two, three are not related except by their sequence, and normally that sequence is arbitrary. If the sentences within a paragraph or if several paragraphs have no other relation than that of being in a list, then what may seem neatly organized is, in fact, loose and slack and in need of care. In the paper on *Hamlet* all the items could be rearranged and the same point could be made, because as these items stand, they are just thrown together any which way. This means that the author thinks or finds the items in *Hamlet* equally disorganized, for he asks nothing more of the play than that it be there somewhere.

Nor is the problem altered when the subject changes from literary characters to something else. What were the causes of World War II? How is an Israeli kibbutz organized? Was Emerson a Calvinist? The answers to each of these is easily reducible to a list, although none has to be so reduced. And the "compare and contrast" questions often invite papers that look like big swinging gates: compare Jesus' and Socrates' ideas of the right relation of the individual to authority, contrast the agricultural programs of the USA and the USSR. Again, papers on these subjects do not have to give in to the temptation to outline and thereby achieve disorganization. But if the writer has one paragraph or group of paragraphs on one side of his comparison and another paragraph or group of paragraphs on the other side, the chances are very good the result is really two papers connected in the middle by an "on the other hand," or an "unlike Socrates, Jesus . . ." Or the writer might use a common term but use it in different ways—use "authority," for example, in the case of Socrates to mean state authority and in the case of Jesus to mean divine authority—so that the comparison is one of the apples and oranges variety. Or, to take the opposite fault, it is possible to employ one set of terms for both sides of the comparison but to use terms that give all the advantages to one side. If I compare Jesus and Socrates as religious leaders, for instance, I am cheating; Jesus was a great religious leader, while Socrates made no effort to be one at all. This fault arises especially when the writer is asked to say which is the better of two things; the easiest way to solve the problem is by an unfair comparison.

This does not mean that outlining is always fatal. In long

[83]

papers especially, it is often essential to get some skeleton organization clear before beginning. The fault, obviously, never lies in the outline but in the outline maker. The real trouble comes when a writer feels that once he has made his outline his organizational problems are over. In fact, they have barely begun, because at best most outlines state potential relationships. To say, for instance, that x comes under the heading of y certainly begins to relate x and y, but if the exact nature of that relationship is not explored, and if the relation of x to x' and to z and the relation of all three to y is not made precise, then the original statement that x comes under the heading of y will probably remain vague. We are brought back to the original idea, that organization is first a matter of relating things within and between sentences and then a matter of large-scale form. Outline makers can delude themselves into thinking they have done something they have not yet done, whereas the writer who just starts in and keeps asking himself how things go together is less likely to be under any illusions about what he has and hasn't done.

As people use the words "logic" and "logical" to mean almost anything they please, I cannot hope to treat the many things implied in its name in one place. As with outlines, the complaint against people who "use logic" is not with the logic but with the use. A well-trained philosopher can do wonderful things by taking a good, well-meaning paragraph and unpacking it so as to show the kinds of logic and illogic used in it. He can show the extent to which most of our sense of argument is not logical but analogical, and how a great many people think they have proved something when, in fact, they have only found an analogue for it. But we all are not good or well-trained philosophers, and often many strange misdemeanors are committed in the name of being logical.

A lot of people use deductive logic when they try to seem knowing as a means of avoiding the complications of a particular problem.

All men are mortal.
Socrates is a man.
Socrates is mortal.

[84]

This is the classic syllogism, and it is just fine as long as all you want to show is that Socrates is mortal. But it does not take much reflection to know that to say that says little. In a dressed up form, a syllogism can look like this:

Every action, according to Newton, causes an equal and opposite reaction. This is something that apparently the college and university rebels do not fully realize. When they make demands that they know are outrageous, they seek to provoke faculties and administrations into conceding more than they really want to give away. But instead of getting what they want, the student revolutionaries usually do not get what they want. Instead they get a violent reaction from alumni, the press, and state legislatures, all of which suddenly become stubborn in the face of the demands of the revolutionaries.

That paragraph is not, on its surface, at all simplistic, the way "all-men-are-mortal" syllogisms tend to be. Indeed, you can hear arguments like the above in a great many quarters. The form is syllogistic: the major premise is that every action has an equal and opposite reaction; the minor premise is that student revolutionaries are acting; the conclusion is that what they achieve is an equal and opposite reaction from those as much on the right wing as the students are on the left.

It is not the logic of this that is at fault; it is the phony use of logic. What the paragraph asserts may well be true, but if it is true, it certainly has not been proven logically, nor would it be any more logical if the argument above were expanded, as such arguments often are, to take up many pages instead of one paragraph. That every action causes an equal and opposite reaction is indeed a Newtonian law of motion, and for the moment we can assume that Newton's law is true enough for physical bodies. But the paragraph is not about physical bodies but social groups, and at no point after the middle of its second sentence are its assertions more than analogical. They assume, but they do not (and cannot) prove logically, that social groups react as physical bodies do. If two balls on a pool table collide, the impact of one ball on the other causes something easily describable as an equal and opposite reaction; the ball that is struck moves away from the ball that strikes it in an opposite direction. But left-wing college revolutionaries and right-wing reactionary groups do not operate under the same laws as the two balls on the pool table. Often they may react *like* the two balls, and often it may seem that we can predict the response of one group if the other group moves. But physical bodies and social groups can only be related analogically, not logically, so that the maker of the analogue has no right to claim anything like logical proof for his analogical assertions.

The form of the syllogism is appealing. It looks good, and it seems to convince unwary people. But the form of the logic, like the form of other outlines, deceives writer and reader, and keeps both from looking into the facts of the case. In many cases, undoubtedly, revolutionary action has spurred on or encouraged right-wing reaction, and the reader of the above argument is encouraged to supply appropriate examples from his own experience to support the analogue. But even if in every known case social groups did respond like physical bodies, that would not make the paragraph any more logical or valid, even though it would make it much more convincing. No matter what else is true, the proof of the assertion cannot lie in its logic but in the number and quality of examples that can be offered so as to make the analogue convincing. Most of the time, however, people who accept the shell of the syllogism ask for little more than that, and so come to accept as true that which is only possible or perhaps likely. The logical outline constantly has this tendency to delude its maker into thinking he has done more, proven more, than in fact he has, and often a long and elaborate argument is made to rest on a "logic" that is, in fact, only a suggestive analogue or metaphor.

The other major abuse of logic comes in the use of murky or vague terms, such as the following:

> Passionate men tend to become violent when they are frustrated, and Heathcliff is no exception. When Catherine apparently rejects him, Heathcliff reacts violently by leaving home.

The argument here could be buttressed a great deal with example and quotation, but the syllogism would remain the same: the major premise is that passionate men become violent when frustrated; its minor premise is that Heathcliff is a passionate man; its conclusion is that when Heathcliff becomes frustrated he will become violent. The difficulty here is not the leakiness of the logic but the vagueness of the terms: both "passionate" and "violent" are allowed to stand here, as they are so often in our discourse, without clarification. In this particular case, the passionate quality of the individual is not in question. But when the author says that Heathcliff's leaving home is a violent reaction, he really is asking us to believe the syllogism so we will believe in the appropriateness of the terms. Heathcliff does indeed leave home, but it is hard to claim that that is a "violent" response; "sudden" is perhaps the better term. If the author is trying to prove that Heathcliff is passionate by offering as evidence the suddenness of his departure, he may well be right, but he has not logically proven his case.

The two examples offered here are short, but it isn't hard to see that their arguments could easily be expanded greatly. Indeed, the effect of such expansion often is to encourage the writer into thinking he is being more logical when, in fact, he is only being more expansive. If his logic is leaky or if his terms are vague and squishy, he may, by the opulence of his surrounding statements, feel he has proven something when he may only be covering up a phony argument. But notice I say "may be" covering up. In fact he may be right, but if he is right, it is not because he is being logical. Often the rightness of a given argument is disturbed by an elaborate wrongness of method; more often a shaky or partially true argument is given a kind of illegitimate legitimacy by the smokescreen of a logical structure.

Introductions and Conclusions

Perhaps nowhere is the tendency of rules to countermand reason more prevalent than in the writing of introductions and conclusions. We all know what these are, and if we are in any doubt the handbooks can tell us.

Introductions introduce, of course, and conclusions conclude. The best simple test of whether these putative events in fact take place is to ask these questions: is the introduction anything

[87]

more than a clearing of the throat? is the conclusion anything more than a late rehearsal?

Introductions can be of any length, from a sentence to a whole book, and obviously the shorter the paper the shorter the introduction. A lot of papers, however, don't need introductions at all, in the usual sense, for the simple reason that what they are going to do will be clear from their first sentence anyway, in which case introductions are redundant, throat-clearing. I am, for instance, fond of an assignment that goes like this: "Look at Hamlet's speech 'To be or not to be' and describe it so as to make clear Hamlet's situation at this point in the play." For a short paper I might stop with that. For a longer paper I might proceed: "Now look at Hamlet's speech to Horatio at the end of the play and describe it so as to make clear Hamlet's situation here. Then say what happens to Hamlet as he moves from one situation to the other." For either the short paper or the longer paper, no introduction is needed. Look at these two possible openings:

> "To be or not to be" shows Hamlet at his lowest moment in the play, contemplating suicide and so far removed from the world around him that, in this speech, he often seems unable or uninterested in distinguishing suicide from murder.

> The character of Hamlet has fascinated audience and readers for almost four centuries, and no final solution to the problems of his character has ever been made, and probably none ever will be. If we look at his speeches and movement from Act III to Act V, we may be able to see why he is so enigmatic and difficult to grasp.

The first is not an introduction at all, only a beginning. The second is not very long, to be sure—most efforts that begin like this are much longer—but it is quite unnecessary. Both beginnings, notice, like the beginnings of most papers, assume an audience that knows the question asked, and neither, therefore, would be appropriate if the audience had no idea what the writer was going to write about.

But clearly a great many papers do need introductions of some kind. Here are a group, all written in answer to an assignment about four short stories by four different writers:

[88]

The four short stories involved in the writing of this paper are different in many ways. The settings are different—compare Mexico to Kentucky; the characters are different types—a young boy compared to a traveling salesman. The differences seem to overcome the similarities, and this makes for a very difficult essay. Because of this difference, I am going to show the change in character that occurs because of a single event in the life of the character or the result of this change upon the lives of others.

—II—

Through all the stories is an underlying theme expressing the uncertainty or frailty of human judgment. The characters make irrational judgments about people and life, and each becomes aware that he has made a serious mistake. How each of four major characters respond to the discovery of their mistake, and how the four authors respond to their characters, is the subject of this essay.

—III—

Any attempt to write an artistic, specific, concise, and thorough essay on these four stories is, to say the least, difficult. After a first reading, the only similarities they seem to have are that they are published in the same book. However, a similarity does seem to develop in the characters of the stories. If one can say the thoughts and actions of the stories represent the theme, then it is possible for me to advance an overall response and meaning which will apply to all the stories. The idea I will engage is one of character change. In each story the reader can view how a character changes in respect to the situations of life he is brought into.

Of these three opening paragraphs, the second comes closest genuinely to introducing what comes next. The first and the third really are just standing around waiting for it to come time to move on. No one in the world has ever *thought about* writing a sentence like the opening of the first paragraph: "The four short stories involved in the writing of this paper are different in many ways"; the writer is merely thinking he must get underway somehow. So too with the opening of the third: "Any attempt to write an artistic, specific, concise, and thorough essay on these four stories is, to say the least, difficult." It is enough to tempt a retort in the margin like, "And to say the most? One must be obedient, cheerful, brave, clean, and reverent?" These sentences are throat-clearing of the most obvious sort. The second paragraph, on the other hand, is certainly trying to do what an introduction is supposed to do: tell the reader something about what is to follow.

But even the second paragraph shares a defect with the others that indicates that the paper to follow may not be able to avoid paralysis-through-outlining. Introductions are part and parcel of the machinery of outlining, and these three opening paragraphs show how outlines are often instrumental in keeping writers from saying what they want to say. Each writer has chosen to approach the stories in a way congenial to an outline, by finding a common thread or theme in the four stories and sticking to it. But finding such a theme is usually only an exercise in ingenuity, because what is most interesting about four stories by four different writers is probably not what they have in common with each other. But because all stories share some things in common —they are in prose, they have beginnings and endings, characters, scenes, probably a plot and some dialogue—a writer who is anxious to find a common thread or theme hits upon some uninteresting link or thin strand on which he can string his beads: "a change in character that occurs because of a single event in the life of the character," "a character changes in respect to the situations of life he is brought into," "an underlying theme expressing the uncertainty or frailty of human judgment." Such threads will "work," of course, in the dreadful sense that on these strands the papers can be strung and so finished and handed in. But two results of this theme-hunting are almost inevitable: the "theme" is so vague (as in the first two paragraphs) that the writer then writes four isolated essays on four stories with nothing really done to relate them; and the "theme" fits one story or maybe two quite well but not the others, so that stories have to be badly distorted in order to make them all adhere to the outlined theme.

The difficulty I'm speaking of here is not, perhaps, strictly a matter of introductions, but the introduction is the best and easiest place to see such disasters in the making. Throat-clearing is the most obvious sign of a paper that the writer really doesn't want to write at all, or doesn't want to write that way. He sees the laboriousness, and perhaps the silliness, of what he is about to do, and for him the task has become one of just filling up the page. He writes an introduction because he thinks he must, but he hasn't got much to introduce, and so finds himself writing a sentence like "However, a similarity does seem to develop in the characters of the stories," where he is lurching into vague and indecisive action. Unless something happens to shake up such a writer into quite a different state of mind, the paper to follow will be, at best, mechanical and competent and, at worst, more nonsense along the lines of "does seem to develop."

The best advice to writers about introductions is never to start with one. It may turn out that the paper has so many intricate twists or enough unexpected lines of development or is simply long enough to demand a small guidebook at its beginning, but that is something that can be decided later, after the shape or shapes of the paper have become clear. The man told to write a paper on four short stories probably should sit down and write four separate papers, not necessarily connected with each other, on the stories. Let each paper try to say what seems most worth saying: about one story that it is a fraud, about another that it has a great ending, about a third that it has a haunting character, about a fourth that it is obscure. Let no worry be paid to organization of the paper as a whole until the four separate papers are done. In most cases, a means of organizing the whole will appear in the process of writing the separate papers; in some others, a quick reading of the four will reveal honest ways of relating them; if one or more of the separate papers resists decent shaping, the best thing to do is not to lie but to say that the generalizations just don't apply to this particular story, at which point it can be decided if an introduction is necessary. Often, especially with papers under a thousand words (or four typed pages), introductions are only a nuisance. In any event, by not starting with an introduction a writer is forced to do his relating where it counts, sentence-by-sentence, so as to keep his sense of direction clear to his reader. It is a neat challenge: can you make your direction and your organization clear without announcing what they are at the beginning?

Conclusions usually are treated as a mirror image of introductions, but, in fact, they are far more important. All too often conclusions look like this:

> In this paper I have attempted to show how four different stories show how the character of man can easily be molded through the sequence of a single event. In the first three cases the character was changed through an event of his own doing; in the fourth he was affected by a character change in others. This easily changing manner of man shows that man is pliable. His character is not rigid, but is made of clay.

If you look back to the three introductory paragraphs quoted earlier, you probably can spot the one to which this is the concluding mirror. To some, the idea that a conclusion resembles an introduction is neat, pleasant, and comforting, and to have a conclusion like this one gives the impression of having finished the job off. "The man knew where he wanted to go and got there," is perhaps praise of the writer of such a conclusion. But surely that way of speaking assumes a paper is rather like a quarter-mile track, and that a writer is or should be rather like a runner—fast, determined, efficient, with no nonsense. In other words, conclusions which really are just mirrors of their introductions *add* nothing. They only repeat and summarize, and usually the conclusions they come to are foregone. After all, if you can match a conclusion with its introduction, that means, in effect, the writer has told you enough at the beginning so that the whole paper is only a working out of its opening statement. Papers like that usually are like neatly wrapped packages, and the conclusion is only an ornamental bow placed on top. Take the conclusion above away from the paper and what is lost?—a sense of rounding off prettily.

But nothing else, because the conclusion that only repeats what is said earlier obviously does not represent the farthest reach of a particular line of thought, nor does it carry the writer out to a point beyond which he cannot go. It turns back inward, toward the paper, and is only formally necessary at best.

[92]

Here is the conclusion to another one of the introductions quoted above:

> Regardless of how well or how poorly they decide what to do, then, people end up lonely. In these stories someone is always thinking that if he could only be richer or more talented he would then be happy. But, in fact, those who get what they want, those who find they cannot have what they want, and those who see their desires are vain all end alike: isolated, lonely, unfulfilled. It is as though the modern short story were constantly at war with the ancient fairy tale, so that the idea of loneliness is as constant in the short story as the idea of living happily ever after was in the fairy tale. On television and in movies we still have fairy tales, but when people try to write literature they know better, or think they do.

In the first three sentences of this paragraph we have what is obviously summary, but even then it is not simply a repetition of the introduction. Beginning with the fourth sentence—"It is as though the modern short story . . ."—we have what seems like something new, as though the conclusion the writer is drawing about these particular stories is then being made the basis for further thought. It is not, perhaps, a great or a greatly original thought, but it is at least an effort to move out and move on, not to turn back. This writer does not talk about "man" in the general sense; he seems to know better than to try to make conclusions about "man" on the basis of four stories. But four stories is a pretty good sampling of stories, and so the writer can safely offer his little generalization about modern stories. Nothing ringing or thundering—that would be to conclude more than is justifiable. The writer takes his material and goes as far as he honestly can with it. The proper analogy for such a procedure is not a quarter-mile track but a path cut through a forest. The writer is going to go as far as he can on the basis of what he can work out from these stories. He doesn't know when he begins just how far he can go, so he sets out, taking the stories as he finds them, concluding what he can from them, then stopping.

It seems to me that the second of these conclusions is or should be no harder to write than the first. It takes no profound insight, no wide ranging expertise, no subtle skill in literary analysis. It is not immensely better than the first, for that matter, but it is better in an important way. That effort in the last two sentences of the second conclusion shows that the writer senses he should not stop thinking until the last word, whereas the writer of the first paper seems to have stopped thinking the moment he worked out his outline. For him the writing of the paper is a process like filling in the blanks of a questionnaire or following the dots.

The distinction I am trying to draw here, however, is really too important to be allowed to rest simply as a matter of one concluding paragraph being better than another. The next section takes up the question of development rather than repetition in more detail. It can be said here, though, that one of the easiest ways to spot a hard-working and thoughtful writer is to look at his opening and closing paragraphs. The standard introduction and conclusion usually bespeak a writer who is trying to write a prepackaged paper, a box neatly tied with pretty ribbon. The good writer does not have to try to avoid standard introductions and conclusions—to try to avoid anything just for the sake of doing so is always silly. Rather, he is different because his introduction and conclusion are following his thoughts instead of fitting those thoughts into mechanical routines.

Development and Repetition

Of all the subjects taken up in this book, this one is perhaps the most difficult to deal with well. Writers learn very early that they should develop their ideas and avoid repetition, but to learn these things as rules and to practice them as part of one's way of writing are very different things. The guidelines are simple enough: keep going, push your ideas, develop them, don't stop until you have to, don't be content with easy and bland conclusions when tougher and more interesting ones are at hand. But those things are not only easier said than done; they are easier said than explained. Here we will have to have some extended quotations, because the arena is not only the paragraph but the extended argument.

[94]

The following papers were all written about a selection from James Baldwin's *The Fire Next Time* that is reprinted below.*

I underwent, during the summer that I became fourteen, a prolonged religious crisis. I use the word "religious" in the common, and arbitrary, sense, meaning that I then discovered God, His saints and angels, and His blazing Hell. And since I had been born in a Christian nation, I accepted this Deity as the only one. I supposed Him to exist only within the walls of a church—in fact, of *our* church—and I also supposed that God and safety were synonymous. The word "safety" brings us to the real meaning of the word "religious" as we use it. Therefore, to state it in another, more accurate way, I became, during my fourteenth year, for the first time in my life, afraid—afraid of the evil within me and afraid of the evil without. What I saw around me that summer in Harlem was what I had always seen; nothing had changed. But now, without any warning, the whores and pimps and racketeers on the Avenue had become a personal menace. It had not before occurred to me that I could become one of them, but now I realized that we had been produced by the same circumstances. Many of my comrades were clearly headed for the Avenue, and my father said that I was headed that way, too. My friends began to drink and smoke, and embarked—at first avid, then groaning—on their sexual careers. Girls, only slightly older than I was, who sang in the choir or taught Sunday school, the children of holy parents, underwent, before my eyes, their incredible metamorphosis, of which the most bewildering aspect was not their budding breasts or their rounding behinds but something deeper and more subtle, in their eyes, their heat, their odor, and the inflection of their voices. Like the strangers on the Avenue, they became, in the twinkling of an eye, unutterably different and fantastically *present*. Owing to the way I had been raised, the abrupt discomfort that all this aroused in me and the fact that I had no idea what my voice or my mind or my body was likely to do next caused me to consider myself one of the most depraved people on earth. Matters were not helped by the fact that these holy girls seemed rather to enjoy my terrified lapses, our grim, guilty, tormented experiments, which were at once as chill and joyless as the Russian steppes and hotter, by far, than all the fires of Hell.

* Reprinted from *The Fire Next Time* by permission of The Dial Press, Inc., and John Farquharson, Ltd. Copyright © 1963, 1962 by James Baldwin.

[95]

Yet there was something deeper than these changes, and less definable, that frightened me. It was real in both the boys and the girls, but it was, somehow, more vivid in the boys. In the case of the girls, one watched them turning into matrons before they had become women. They began to manifest a curious and really rather terrifying single-mindedness. It is hard to say exactly how this was conveyed: something implacable in the set of the lips, something farseeing (seeing what?) in the eyes, some new and crushing determination in the walk, something peremptory in the voice. They did not tease us, the boys, any more; they reprimanded us sharply, saying, "You better be thinking about your soul!" For the girls also saw the evidence on the Avenue, knew what the price would be, for them, of one misstep, knew that they had to be protected and that we were the only protection there was. They understood that they must act as God's decoys, saving the souls of the boys for Jesus and binding the bodies of the boys in marriage. For this was the beginning of our burning time, and "It is better," said St. Paul—who elsewhere, with a most unusual and stunning exactness, described himself as a "wretched man"—"to marry than to burn." And I began to feel in the boys a curious, wary, bewildered despair, as though they were now settling in for the long, hard winter of life. I did not know then what it was that I was reacting to; I put it to myself that they were letting themselves go. In the same way that the girls were destined to gain as much weight as their mothers, the boys, it was clear, would rise no higher than their fathers. School began to reveal itself, therefore, as a child's game that one could not win, and boys dropped out of school and went to work. My father wanted me to do the same. I refused, even though I no longer had any illusions about what an education could do for me; I had already encountered too many college-graduate handymen. My friends were now "downtown," busy, as they put it, "fighting the man." They began to care less about the way they looked, the way they dressed, the things they did; presently, one found them in twos and threes and fours, in a hallway, sharing a jug of wine or a bottle of whiskey, talking, cursing, fighting, sometimes weeping: lost, and unable to say what it was that oppressed them, except that they knew it was "the man"—the white man. And there seemed to be no way whatever to remove this cloud that stood between them and the sun, between them and love and life and power, between them and whatever it was that they wanted. One did not have to be very bright to realize how little one could do to change one's situation; one did not

[96]

have to be abnormally sensitive to be worn down to a cutting edge by the incessant and gratuitous humiliation and danger one encountered every working day, all day long. The humiliation did not apply merely to working days, or workers; I was thirteen and was crossing Fifth Avenue on my way to the Forty-second Street library, and the cop in the middle of the street muttered as I passed him, "Why don't you niggers stay uptown where you belong?" When I was ten, and didn't look, certainly, any older, two policemen amused themselves with me by frisking me, making comic (and terrifying) speculations concerning my ancestry and probable sexual prowess, and for good measure, leaving me flat on my back in one of Harlem's empty lots. Just before and then during the Second World War, many of my friends fled into the service, all to be changed there, and rarely for the better, many to be ruined, and many to die. Others fled to other states and cities—that is, to other ghettos. Some went on wine or whiskey or the needle, and are still on it. And others, like me, fled into the church.

For the wages of sin were visible everywhere, in every wine-stained and urine-splashed hallway, in every clanging ambulance bell, in every scar on the faces of the pimps and their whores, in every helpless, newborn baby being brought into this danger, in every knife and pistol fight on the Avenue, and in every disastrous bulletin: a cousin, mother of six, suddenly gone mad, the children parcelled out here and there; an indestructible aunt rewarded for years of hard labor by a slow, agonizing death in a terrible small room; someone's bright son blown into eternity by his own hand; another turned robber and carried off to jail. It was a summer of dreadful speculations and discoveries, of which these were not the worst. Crime became real, for example —for the first time—not as *a* possibility but as *the* possibility. One would never defeat one's circumstances by working and saving one's pennies; one would never, by working, acquire that many pennies, and, besides, the social treatment accorded even the most successful Negroes proved that one needed, in order to be free, something more than a bank account. One needed a handle, a lever, a means of inspiring fear. It was absolutely clear that the police would whip you and take you in as long as they could get away with it, and that everyone else—house-wives, taxi-drivers, elevator boys, dishwashers, bartenders, law-yers, judges, doctors, and grocers—would never, by the operation of any generous human feeling, cease to use you as an outlet for his frustrations and hostilities. Neither civilized reason nor Christian love would cause any of those people to treat you as they presumably wanted to be treated; only the fear of your power to retaliate would cause them to do that, or to seem to do it, which was (and is) good enough. There appears to be a vast amount of confusion on this point, but I do not know many Negroes who are eager to be "accepted" by white people, still less to be loved by them; they, the blacks, simply don't wish to be beaten over the head by the whites every instant of our brief passage on this planet. White people in this country will have quite enough to do in learning how to accept and love themselves and each other, and when they have achieved this— which will not be tomorrow and may very well be never—the Negro problem will no longer exist, for it will no longer be needed.

People more advantageously placed than we in Harlem were, and are, will no doubt find the psychology and the view of human nature sketched above dismal and shocking in the extreme. But the Negro's experience of the white world cannot possibly create in him any respect for the standards by which the white world claims to live. His own condition is overwhelming proof that white people do not live by these standards. Negro servants have been smuggling odds and ends out of white homes for generations, and white people have been delighted to have them do it, because it has assuaged a dim guilt and testified to the intrinsic superiority of white people. Even the most doltish and servile Negro could scarcely fail to be impressed by the disparity between his situation and that of the people for whom he worked; Negroes who were neither doltish nor servile did not feel that they were doing anything wrong when they robbed white people. In spite of the Puritan-Yankee equation of virtue with well-being, Negroes had excellent reasons for doubting that money was made or kept by any very striking adherence to the Christian virtues; it certainly did not work that way for black Christians. In any case, white people, who had robbed black people of their liberty and who profited by this theft every hour that they lived, had no moral ground on which to stand. They had the judges, the juries, the shotguns, the law— in a word, power. But it was a criminal power, to be feared but not respected, and to be outwitted in any way whatever. And those virtues preached but not practiced by the white world were merely another means of holding Negroes in subjection.

It turned out, then, that summer, that the moral barriers that I had supposed to exist between me and the dangers of a criminal career were so tenuous as to be nearly nonexistent. I certainly could not discover any principled reason for not becoming a criminal, and it is not my poor, God-fearing parents who are to be indicted for the lack but this society. I was icily determined —more determined, really, than I then knew—never to make my peace with the ghetto but to die and go to Hell before I would let any white man spit on me, before I would accept my "place" in this republic. I did not intend to allow the white people of this country to tell me who I was, and limit me that way, and polish me off that way. And yet, of course, at the same time, I *was* being spat on and defined and described and limited, and could have been polished off with no effort whatever. Every Negro boy—in my situation during those years, at least—who reaches this point realizes, at once, profoundly, because he wants to live, that he stands in great peril and must find, with speed, a "thing," a gimmick, to lift him out, to start him on his way. *And it does not matter what the gimmick is.* It was this last realization that terrified me and—since it revealed that the door opened on so many dangers—helped to hurl me into the church. And, by an unforeseeable paradox, it was my career in the church that turned out, precisely, to be my gimmick.

For when I tried to assess my capabilities, I realized that I had almost none. In order to achieve the life I wanted, I had been dealt, it seemed to me, the worst possible hand. I could not become a prizefighter—many of us tried but very few succeeded. I could not sing. I could not dance. I had been well conditioned by the world in which I grew up, so I did not yet dare take the idea of becoming a writer seriously. The only other possibility seemed to involve my becoming one of the sordid people on the Avenue, who were not really as sordid as I then imagined but who frightened me terribly, both because I did not want to live that life and because of what they made me feel. Everything inflamed me, and that was bad enough, but I myself had also become a source of fire and temptation. I had been far too well raised, alas, to suppose that any of the extremely explicit overtures made to me that summer, sometimes by boys and girls but also, more alarmingly, by older men and women, had anything to do with my attractiveness. On the contrary, since the Harlem idea of seduction is, to put it mildly, blunt, whatever these people saw in me merely confirmed my sense of my depravity.

It is certainly sad that the awakening of one's senses should lead to such a merciless judgment of oneself—to say nothing of the time and anguish one spends in the effort to arrive at any other—but it is also inevitable that a literal attempt to mortify the flesh should be made among black people like those with whom I grew up. Negroes in this country—and Negroes do not, strictly or legally speaking, exist in any other—are taught really to despise themselves from the moment their eyes open on the world. This world is white and they are black. White people hold the power, which means that they are superior to blacks (intrinsically, that is: God decreed it so), and the world has innumerable ways of making this difference known and felt and feared. Long before the Negro child perceives this difference, and even longer before he understands it, he has begun to react to it, he has begun to be controlled by it. Every effort made by the child's elders to prepare him for a fate from which they cannot protect him causes him secretly, in terror, to begin to await, without knowing that he is doing so, his mysterious and inexorable punishment. He must be "good" not only in order to please his parents and not only to avoid being punished by them; behind their authority stands another, nameless and impersonal, infinitely harder to please, and bottomlessly cruel. And this filters into the child's consciousness through his parents' tone of voice as he is being exhorted, punished, or loved; in the sudden, uncontrollable note of fear heard in his mother's or his father's voice when he has strayed beyond some particular boundary. He does not know what the boundary is, and he can get no explanation of it, which is frightening enough, but the fear he hears in the voices of his elders is more frightening still. The fear that I heard in my father's voice, for example, when he realized that I really *believed* I could do anything a white boy could do, and had every intention of proving it, was not at all like the fear I heard when one of us was ill or had fallen down the stairs or strayed too far from the house. It was another fear, a fear that the child, in challenging the white world's assumptions, was putting himself in the path of destruction. A child cannot, thank Heaven, know how vast and how merciless is the nature of power, with what unbelievable cruelty people treat each other. He reacts to the fear in his parents' voices because his parents hold up the world for him and he has no protection without them. I defended myself, as I imagined, against the fear my father made me feel by remembering that he was very old-fashioned. Also, I prided myself on the fact that I already knew how to outwit him. To defend oneself against a fear is simply to insure that one will, one day, be conquered by it; fears must be faced. As for one's wits, it is just not true that one can live by them—not, that is, if one wishes really to live. That summer, in any case, all the fears with which I had grown up, and which were now a part of me and controlled my vision of the world, rose up like a wall between the world and me, and drove me into the church.

As I look back, everything I did seems curiously deliberate, though it certainly did not seem deliberate then. For example, I did not join the church of which my father was a member and in which he preached. My best friend in school, who attended a different church, had already "surrendered his life to the Lord," and he was very anxious about my soul's salvation. (I wasn't, but any human attention was better than none.) One Saturday afternoon, he took me to his church. There were no services that day, and the church was empty, except for some women cleaning and some other women praying. My friend took me into the back room to meet his pastor—a woman. There she sat, in her robes, smiling, an extremely proud and handsome woman, with Africa, Europe, and the America of the American Indian blended in her face. She was perhaps forty-five or fifty at this time, and in our world she was a very celebrated woman. My friend was about to introduce me when she looked at me and smiled and said, "Whose little boy are you?" Now this, unbelievably, was precisely the phrase used by pimps and racketeers on the Avenue when they suggested, both humorously and intensely, that I "hang out" with them. Perhaps part of the terror they had caused me to feel came from the fact that I unquestionably wanted to be *somebody's* little boy. I was so frightened, and at the mercy of so many conundrums, that inevitably, that summer, *someone* would have taken me over; one doesn't, in Harlem, long remain standing on any auction block. It was my good luck—perhaps—that I found myself in the church racket instead of some other, and surrendered to a spiritual seduction long before I came to any carnal knowledge. For when the pastor asked me, with that marvellous smile, "Whose little boy are you?" my heart replied at once, "Why, yours."

The summer wore on, and things got worse. I became more guilty and more frightened, and kept all this bottled up inside me, and naturally, inescapably, one night, when this woman had finished preaching, everything came roaring, screaming, crying out, and I fell to the ground before the altar. It was the strangest sensation I have ever had in my life—up to that time, or since. I had not known that it was going to happen, or that it could happen.

One moment I was on my feet, singing and clapping and, at the same time, working out in my head the plot of a play I was working on then; the next moment, with no transition, no sensation of falling, I was on my back, with the light beating down into my face and all the vertical saints above me. I did not know what I was doing down so low, or how I had got there. And the anguish that filled me cannot be described. It moved in me like one of those floods that devastate counties, tearing everything down, tearing children from their parents and lovers from each other, and making everything an unrecognizable waste. All I really remember is the pain, the unspeakable pain; it was as though I were yelling up to Heaven and Heaven would not hear me. And if Heaven would not hear me, if love could not descend from Heaven—to wash me, to make me clean—then utter disaster was my portion. Yes, it does indeed mean something—something unspeakable—to be born, in a white country, an Anglo-Teutonic, antisexual country, black. You very soon, without knowing it, give up all hope of communion. Black people, mainly, look down or look up but do not look at each other, not at you, and white people, mainly, look away. And the universe is simply a sounding drum; there is no way, no way whatever, so it seemed then and has sometimes seemed since, to get through a life, to love your wife and children, or your friends, or your mother and father, or to be loved. The universe, which is not merely the stars and the moon and the planets, flowers, grass, and trees, but *other people*, has evolved no terms for your existence, has made no room for you, and if love will not swing wide the gates, no other power will or can. And if one despairs—as who has not? —of human love, God's love alone is left. But God—and I felt this even then, so long ago, on that tremendous floor, unwillingly —is white. And if His love was so great, and if He loved all His children, why were we, the blacks, cast down so far? Why? In spite of all I said thereafter, I found no answer on the floor —not *that* answer, anyway—and I was on the floor all night. Over me, to bring me "through," the saints sang and rejoiced and prayed. And in the morning, when they raised me, they told me that I was "saved."

Well, indeed I was, in a way, for I was utterly drained and exhausted, and released, for the first time, from all my guilty torment. I was aware then only of my relief. For many years, I could not ask myself why human relief had to be achieved in a fashion at once so pagan and so desperate—in a fashion at once so unspeakably old and so unutterably new. And by the time I was able to ask myself this question, I was also able to see that the principles governing the rites and customs of the churches in which I grew up did not differ from the principles governing the rites and customs of other churches, white. The principles were Blindness, Loneliness, and Terror, the first principle necessarily and actively cultivated in order to deny the two others. I would love to believe that the principles were Faith, Hope, and Charity, but this is clearly not so for most Christians, or for what we call the Christian world.

I was saved. But at the same time, out of a deep, adolescent cunning I do not pretend to understand, I realized immediately that I could not remain in the church merely as another worshipper. I would have to give myself something to do, in order not to be too bored and find myself among all the wretched unsaved of the Avenue. And I don't doubt that I also intended to best my father on his own ground. Anyway, very shortly after I joined the church, I became a preacher—a Young Minister—and I remained in the pulpit for more than three years. My youth quickly made me a much bigger drawing card than my father. I pushed this advantage ruthlessly, for it was the most effective means I had found of breaking his hold over me. That was the most frightening time of my life, and quite the most dishonest, and the resulting hysteria lent great passion to my sermons—for a while. I relished the attention and the relative immunity from punishment that my new status gave me, and I relished, above all, the sudden right to privacy. It had to be recognized, after all, that I was still a schoolboy, with my schoolwork to do, and I was also expected to prepare at least one sermon a week. During what we may call my heyday, I preached much more often than that. This meant that there were hours and even whole days when I could not be interrupted—not even by my father. I had immobilized him. It took rather more time for me to realize that I had also immobilized myself, and had escaped from nothing whatever.

The church was very exciting. It took a long time for me to disengage myself from this excitement, and on the blindest, most visceral level, I never really have, and never will. There is no music like that music, no drama like the drama of the saints rejoicing, the sinners moaning, the tambourines racing, and all those voices coming together and crying holy unto the Lord. There is still, for me, no pathos quite like the pathos of those multicolored, worn, somehow triumphant and transfigured faces, speaking from the depths of a visible, tangible, continuing despair of the goodness of the Lord. I have never seen anything to equal the fire and excitement that sometimes, without warning, fill a church, causing the church, as Leadbelly and so many others have testified, to "rock." Nothing that has happened to me since equals the power and the glory that I sometimes felt when, in the middle of a sermon, I knew that I was somehow, by some miracle, really carrying, as they said, "the Word"— when the church and I were one. Their pain and their joy were mine, and mine were theirs—they surrendered their pain and joy to me, I surrendered mine to them—and their cries of "Amen!" and "Hallelujah!" and "Yes, Lord!" and "Praise His name!" and "Preach it, brother!" sustained and whipped on my solos until we all became equal, wringing wet, singing and dancing, in anguish and rejoicing, at the foot of the altar. It was, for a long time, in spite of—or, not inconceivably, because of —the shabbiness of my motives, my only sustenance, my meat and drink. I rushed home from school, to the church, to the altar, to be alone there, to commune with Jesus, my dearest Friend, who would never fail me, who knew all the secrets of my heart. Perhaps He did, but I didn't, and the bargain we struck, actually, down there at the foot of the cross, was that He would never let me find out.

He failed His bargain. He was a much better Man than I took Him for. It happened, as things do, imperceptibly, in many ways at once. I date it—the slow crumbling of my faith, the pulverization of my fortress—from the time, about a year after I had begun to preach, when I began to read again. I justified this desire by the fact that I was still in school, and I began, fatally, with Dostoevski. By this time, I was in a high school that was predominantly Jewish. This meant that I was surrounded by people who were, by definition, beyond any hope of salvation, who laughed at the tracts and leaflets I brought to school, and who pointed out that the Gospels had been written long after the death of Christ. This might not have been so distressing if it had not forced me to read the tracts and leaflets myself, for they were indeed, unless one believed their message already, impossible to believe. I remember feeling dimly that there was a kind of blackmail in it. People, I felt, ought to love the Lord *because* they loved Him, and not because they were afraid of going to Hell. I was forced, reluctantly, to realize that the Bible itself had been written by men, and translated by men out of languages I could not read, and I was already, without quite admitting it to myself, terribly involved with the effort of putting words on paper. Of course, I had the rebuttal ready: These men had all been operating under divine inspiration. *Had* they? *All* of them? And I also knew by now, alas, far more about divine inspiration than I dared admit, for I knew how I worked myself up into my own visions, and how frequently—indeed, incessantly —the visions God granted to me differed from the visions He granted to my father. I did not understand the dreams I had at night, but I knew that they were not holy. For that matter, I knew that my waking hours were far from holy. I spent most of my time in a state of repentance for things I had vividly desired to do but had not done. The fact that I was dealing with Jews brought the whole question of color, which I had been desperately avoiding, into the terrified center of my mind. I realized that the Bible had been written by white men. I knew that, according to many Christians, I was a descendant of Ham, who had been cursed, and that I was therefore predestined to be a slave. This had nothing to do with anything I was, or contained, or could become; my fate had been sealed forever, from the beginning of time. And it seemed, indeed, when one looked out over Christendom, that this was what Christendom effectively believed. It was certainly the way it behaved. I remembered the Italian priests and bishops blessing Italian boys who were on their way to Ethiopia.

Again, the Jewish boys in high school were troubling because I could find no point of connection between them and the Jewish pawnbrokers and landlords and grocery-store owners in Harlem. I knew that these people were Jews—God knows I was told it often enough—but I thought of them only as white. Jews, as such, until I got to high school, were all incarcerated in the Old Testament, and their names were Abraham, Moses, Daniel, Ezekiel, and Job, and Shadrach, Meshach, and Abednego. It was bewildering to find them so many miles and centuries out of Egypt, and so far from the fiery furnace. My best friend in high school was a Jew. He came to our house once, and afterward my father asked, as he asked about everyone, "Is he a Christian?" —by which he meant "Is he saved?" I really do not know whether my answer came out of innocence or venom, but I said coldly, "No. He's Jewish." My father slammed me across the face with his great palm, and in that moment everything flooded back—all the hatred and all the fear, and the depth of a merciless resolve to kill my father rather than allow my father to kill me —and I knew that all those sermons and tears and all that repentance and rejoicing had changed nothing. I wondered if

I was expected to be glad that a friend of mine, or anyone, was to be tormented forever in Hell, and I also thought, suddenly, of the Jews in another Christian nation, Germany. They were not so far from the fiery furnace after all, and my best friend might have been one of them. I told my father, "He's a better Christian than you are," and walked out of the house. The battle between us was in the open, but that was all right; it was almost a relief. A more deadly struggle had begun.

Being in the pulpit was like being in the theatre; I was behind the scenes and knew how the illusion was worked. I knew the other ministers and knew the quality of their lives. And I don't mean to suggest by this the "Elmer Gantry" sort of hypocrisy concerning sensuality; it was a deeper, deadlier, and more subtle hypocrisy than that, and a little honest sensuality, or a lot, would have been like water in an extremely bitter desert. I knew how to work on a congregation until the last dime was surrendered—it was not very hard to do—and I knew where the money for "the Lord's work" went. I knew, though I did not wish to know it, that I had no respect for the people with whom I worked. I could not have said it then, but I also knew that if I continued I would soon have no respect for myself. And the fact that I was "the young Brother Baldwin" increased my value with those same pimps and racketeers who had helped to stampede me into the church in the first place. They still saw the little boy they intended to take over. They were waiting for me to come to my senses and realize that I was in a very lucrative business. They knew that I did not yet realize this, and also that I had not yet begun to suspect where my own needs, *coming up* (they were very patient), could drive me. They themselves did know the score, and they knew that the odds were in their favor. And, really, I knew it, too. I was even lonelier and more vulnerable than I had been before. And the blood of the Lamb had not cleansed me in any way whatever. I was just as black as I had been the day that I was born. Therefore, when I faced a congregation, it began to take all the strength I had not to stammer, not to curse, not to tell them to throw away their Bibles and get off their knees and go home and organize, for example, a rent strike. When I watched all the children, their copper, brown, and beige faces staring up at me as I taught Sunday school, I felt that I was committing a crime in talking about the gentle Jesus, in telling them to reconcile themselves to their misery on earth in order to gain the crown of eternal life. Were only Negroes to gain this crown? Was Heaven, then, to be merely another ghetto? Perhaps I might have been able to reconcile myself even to this if I had been able to believe that there was any loving-kindness to be found in the haven I represented. But I had been in the pulpit too long and I had seen too many monstrous things. I don't refer merely to the glaring fact that the minister eventually acquires houses and Cadillacs while the faithful continue to scrub floors and drop their dimes and quarters and dollars into the plate. I really mean that there was no love in the church. It was a mask for hatred and self-hatred and despair. The transfiguring power of the Holy Ghost ended when the service ended, and salvation stopped at the church door. When we were told to love everybody, I had thought that that meant *everybody*. But no. It applied only to those who believed as we did, and it did not apply to white people at all. I was told by a minister, for example, that I should never, on any public conveyance, under any circumstances, rise and give my seat to a white woman. White men never rose for Negro women. Well, that was true enough, in the main—I saw his point. But what was the point, the purpose, of *my* salvation if it did not permit me to behave with love toward others, no matter how they behaved toward me? What others did was their responsibility, for which they would answer when the judgment trumpet sounded. But what *I* did was *my* responsibility, and I would have to answer, too—unless, of course, there was also in Heaven a special dispensation for the benighted black, who was not to be judged in the same way as other human beings, or angels. It probably occurred to me around this time that the vision people hold of the world to come is but a reflection, with predictable wishful distortions, of the world in which they live. And this did not apply only to Negroes, who were no more "simple" or "spontaneous" or "Christian" than anybody else—who were merely more oppressed. In the same way that we, for white people, were the descendants of Ham, and were cursed forever, white people were, for us, the descendants of Cain. And the passion with which we loved the Lord was a measure of how deeply we feared and distrusted and, in the end, hated almost all strangers, always, and avoided and despised ourselves.

But I cannot leave it at that; there is more to it than that. In spite of everything, there was in the life I fled a zest and a joy and a capacity for facing and surviving disaster that are very moving and very rare. Perhaps we were, all of us—pimps, whores, racketeers, church members, and children—bound together by the nature of our oppression, the specific and peculiar complex of risks we had to run; if so, within these limits we sometimes achieved with each other a freedom that was close to love. I remember, anyway, church suppers and outings, and, later, after I left the church, rent and waistline parties where rage and sorrow sat in the darkness and did not stir, and we ate and drank and talked and laughed and danced and forgot all about "the man." We had the liquor, the chicken, the music, and each other, and had no need to pretend to be what we were not. This is the freedom that one hears in some gospel songs, for example, and in jazz. In all jazz, and especially in the blues, there is something tart and ironic, authoritative and double-edged. White Americans seem to feel that happy songs are *happy* and sad songs are *sad,* and that, God help us, is exactly the way most white Americans sing them—sounding, in both cases, so helplessly, defenselessly fatuous that one dare not speculate on the temperature of the deep freeze from which issue their brave and sexless little voices. Only people who have been "down the line," as the song puts it, know what this music is about. I think it was Big Bill Broonzy who used to sing "I Feel So Good," a really joyful song about a man who is on his way to the railroad station to meet his girl. She's coming home. It is the singer's incredibly moving exuberance that makes one realize how leaden the time must have been while she was gone. There is no guarantee that she will stay this time, either, as the singer clearly knows, and, in fact, she has not yet actually arrived. Tonight, or tomorrow, or within the next five minutes, he may very well be singing "Lonesome in My Bedroom," or insisting, "Ain't we, ain't we, going to make it all right? Well, if we don't today, we will tomorrow night." White Americans do not understand the depths out of which such an ironic tenacity comes, but they suspect that the force is sensual, and they are terrified of sensuality and do not any longer understand it. The word "sensual" is not intended to bring to mind quivering dusky maidens or priapic black studs. I am referring to something much simpler and much less fanciful. To be sensual, I think, is to respect and rejoice in the force of life, of life itself, and to be *present* in all that one does, from the effort of loving to the breaking of bread. It will be a great day for America, incidentally, when we begin to eat bread again, instead of the blasphemous and tasteless foam rubber that we have substituted for it. And I am not being frivolous now, either. Something very sinister happens to the people of a country when they begin to distrust their own reactions as

deeply as they do here, and become as joyless as they have become. It is this individual uncertainty on the part of white
American men and women, this inability to renew themselves
at the fountain of their own lives, that makes the discussion, let
alone elucidation, of any conundrum—that is, any reality—so
supremely difficult. The person who distrusts himself has no
touchstone for reality—for this touchstone can be only oneself.
Such a person interposes between himself and reality nothing
less than a labyrinth of attitudes. And these attitudes, furthermore, though the person is usually unaware of it (is unaware of
so much!), are historical and public attitudes. They do not relate
to the present any more than they relate to the person. Therefore, whatever white people do not know about Negroes reveals, precisely and inexorably, what they do not know about
themselves.

The papers that follow were written for a quite general assignment on the role of the church in Baldwin's life and in the
lives of other blacks in Harlem, relating that to Baldwin's sense
of a black man's life in white America. For our purposes it does
not matter whether the paper fulfills the assignment; what I
want to discuss is the way each paper seeks to develop its ideas,
the way each sentence and paragraph does or does not build
from those preceding. The first paper isn't even about Baldwin,
but no matter. It is a good place to start.

—I—

Prejudice is difficult to discuss. A great deal of American prejudice against Negroes comes from parental influences. In most
cases, no Negro has ever done harm to a prejudiced person.
When asked why they hate Negroes, most people cannot give
a good answer; sometimes they talk on and on, but all their
"reasoning" tells you is the cause of their prejudice—that they
had been taught to think that way when quite young. Someone
created the myths about Negroes long ago, and they have simply
been handed down from generation to generation.

Almost all anyone learns comes from his parents, our first
teachers, and from them we learn about the world. We think
what they want us to think about anything unknown. Later on
in school we learn from other adults. Our teachers and their attitudes also have an effect. If a child never comes in contact

with Negroes, of course, he can know only what someone else tells him, right or wrong. Prejudiced parents and prejudiced teachers mean prejudiced children, especially when the adults make no effort to hide their feelings. When a child becomes a man, he has a set response to Negroes, and unless he realizes this, there is little hope for his ever feeling any different.

Sometimes prejudice is more hidden, but it is no less effective for that reason. Indeed, when parents do not know they are infecting their children, the result can be worse, and both parents and children do not realize their prejudice.

If only the guilty mothers, fathers, and others would realize what they are doing and let a child grow up and form his own opinions from his own experience with people different from himself, there would not be as much hatred, as much discrimination, or as much need for mass rioting.

This may seem like an extreme example, but it is not, as anyone who has written or read English papers can attest. It could even be praised for being literate, straightforward, unentangled. But, in fact, it really is only one sentence written over and over and over until, in desperation (it would seem), that one sentence is flatly contradicted at the end.

The "logic" can be established by a simple syllogism:

Children learn what they learn from their parents and teachers.
Many parents and teachers are prejudiced against Negroes.
Many children are prejudiced.

A syllogism, by its very nature, deals in the irrefutable and obvious, and a paper that devotes itself to stating and restating a syllogism can never be more than commonplace and obvious. The first sentence of the paper says it all, or would say it if it were properly combined with the second: "Much of the prejudice against Negroes in our country is the result of parental influence upon children and not the result of any wrong done to these children by Negroes." There it is. As an assertion it has the hollow ring of the self-evident, but it is true enough and out of this a paper could be developed. The ways in which a child can gain a fully formed and almost totally ignorant racial consciousness at an early age are many, varied, interesting, and of obviously vital concern. There is much that could be done here, and the writer could proceed by writing out of his own experience, out of his knowledge of the experience of those around him, out of what he reads or sees on television. The fact that the opening assertion isn't interesting or startling by itself is not particularly damaging.

Indeed, in the first paragraph the writer begins, for a moment, to move: "When asked why they hate Negroes, most people cannot give a good answer. Sometimes they talk on and on, but all their 'reasoning' tells you is the cause of their prejudice—that they had been taught to think that way when quite young." This is really the decisive moment in the paper. Up until the dash there is hope for development, but after the dash the hope must go. The sentence begins by describing any person's struggle to explain his reasons for deep and strong but not easily explainable feelings; people talk and talk and they "reason," but what comes clear is that they have no "reason" except a strong sense that what they say is true. Such moments of talking and "reasoning" can be exciting and painful and sad, and had the writer gone on to construct or reconstruct such a moment, he would have done much. But no, the last clause, after the dash, does not move us out, but back, to the original assertion in its flat and self-evident state. How does one "learn" from someone's reasoning that he is prejudiced from childhood? How does one identify a prejudice anyway, in oneself or in someone else? A difficult question, surely, and one that, if intelligently asked and diligently pursued, usually leads to some complex and tentative answers. But here all that is ignored or, more likely, not even thought of, and the result, as so often happens, is repetition.

By the beginning of the second paragraph, there is no doubt left: "Almost all anyone learns comes from his parents. They are our first teachers, and from them we learn about the world." What has happened? The writer, instead of becoming more specific, has become more abstract, more self-evident, more obvious. No one is going to quarrel much with the opening assertion, and to repeat it here with the few particulars about prejudice taken out leads to truisms: teachers have an effect on children; secondhand knowledge is secondhand knowledge; what a child learns he will continue to believe until he sees a reason not to. Everything has collapsed inside the mind of the writer, and he is only filling up pages. But the odd and perhaps the beautiful thing about such writing is that very often, in ways almost hidden from view, the writer knows he is being silly, writing automatically, repeating himself blue in the face, and he will reveal this knowledge unwittingly. Look at the last paragraph here: "If only guilty mothers, fathers, and others would realize what they are doing and let a child grow up and form his own opinions . . ." It is dumb, pathetically so. He has, after all, already said that a child has no chance to avoid learning from his parents, and presumably parents have no choice but to teach their children. It is "natural," as he says. If so, then the "If only . . ." business is unnatural as well as impossible.

The technical term for that last paragraph is "incoherent," but that is not really the point about it. It is almost certainly the work of someone who simply has paid no attention to what he has been saying all along. If told he has repeated himself a dozen times and then contradicted his self-evident proposition, he would almost certainly be indignant. But that, really, is the point about the paper—it isn't a paper at all, only a bloated sentence. Having failed to ask himself where he *could* go with his subject, he inevitably went nowhere with it.

Next we have a quite different sort of paper, one that seems both more and less able to develop itself into something interesting.

—*II*—

"A mask for hatred, self-hatred, and love," a place where love exists only inside of it and stops when one leaves, and a racket. This is Baldwin's portrayal of the church.

Baldwin went to the church to escape the evils of life and to discover loving, but he found only people going to church from fear of going to Hell. He also found that the "basic principles governing the rites and customs of the white peoples' churches were the same principles governing the rites and customs of the Negro churches"—these principles being "blindness, loneliness, and terror" rather than "faith, hope, and charity." "Love thy neighbor" meant "Love only those who belong to this church."

Throughout America, the church is a "mask for hatred, self-hatred, and love" in the sense that white people don't get along with other whites or with the Negro people; the Negroes can't get along with other Negroes, and neither can get along when the races are mixed. The Negro and the white go to church because they have the feeling this will make them better men. What they refuse ever to recognize is that their faith in the church will help them become better men, only if they are willing to do the hard work. The church is an institution of love as long as there is a preacher preaching a sermon. People, Negro and white, go to church, once a week, integrated or segregated. While there, they are very friendly to one another, but as soon as they step out of the church door and meet someone who is not of the same race, do they look at him with love? No. When a white man sees a Negro, he blames him for all the troubles of the society and fears him for all the power he could one day have. However, when a Negro sees a white man, he hates him because the white man will not give him equal power and he fears him because he knows the power of the whites and knows whites will do terrible things they would not do to other whites.

Rather than a church being a place for "faith, hope, and charity," it has become a place of "blindness, loneliness, and terror" in the sense that the majority of the people go to church because it is the "right thing to do" or because, if they don't, people will look down on them. Some see the first principle of the church: blindness. Although people go to church, they forget the real reason behind the church: love. The principle of loneliness shows that people go to church trying to find love, just as Baldwin had done, but they always find there is no real love. The third principle of terror shows that people believe there is a God who will someday judge them, and they are afraid. Consequently, they go to church to protect themselves from going to Hell.

The church, the one place where there should be love and equality between fellow men, has no more real love than the society in which it stands. As Baldwin says:

> *The universe, which is not merely the stars and the moon and the planets, flowers, grass, and trees, but* other people, *has evolved no terms for your existence, has made no room for you, and if love will not swing wide the gates, no other power will or can.*

People do not even know how to love each other in a complex, modern world like ours if they can't find the real meaning of love through the church. This ties in directly with Baldwin's main view toward the Negro versus white dispute:

> *There appears to be a vast amount of confusion on this point, but I do not know many Negroes who are eager to be loved by them; they, the blacks, simply don't wish to be beaten over the heads by whites every instant of our brief passage on this planet. White people in this country will have quite enough to do in learning how to accept and love themselves and each other and when they have achieved this—which will not be tomorrow and may very well be never—the Negro problem will no longer exist, for it will no longer be needed.*

Baldwin means that there is a definite conflict between the white people themselves as seen in church and in other areas of social America. However, the whites feel superior to the Negroes and so they blame this on the Negroes. Therefore, if the white people learn to love each other, "the Negro problem will no longer be needed" because the whites will no longer need to blame the Negroes for this conflict.

The church in our society is falling short of its duty to teach the people to love their fellow men. Therefore, the Negro-white problem will never be solved.

I think most readers will begin by having a good deal more sympathy with this writer than with the first, partly because the troubles he has are so obvious, and because he seems so pathetically unable to solve them. I can imagine a teacher saying of this: "The paper wanders all over the place but makes some very good points."

But, in fact, it doesn't make any very good points. Instead it does what the first paper does, makes the same point over and over. The difference lies in the way this writer seems to be searching for a way to develop his point, whereas the writer of the first paper never even tries. Look at the way the opening sentences of the paper's paragraphs are simple variations on the point most simply made in Baldwin's phrase quoted at the beginning of the paper:

1. "A mask for hatred, self-hatred, and love," a place where love exists only inside of it and stops when one leaves, and a racket.
2. Baldwin went to the church to escape the evils of life, and to

discover loving, but he found only people going to church from fear of going to Hell.

3. Throughout America, the church is a "mask for hatred, self-hatred, and love" in the sense that white people don't get along with other whites or with the Negro people, the Negroes can't get along with other Negroes, and neither can get along when the races are mixed.

4. Rather than a church being a place for "faith, hope, and charity," it has become a place of "blindness, loneliness, and terror . . ."

5. The church, the one place where there should be love and equality between fellow men, has no more real love than the society in which it stands.

6. The church in our society is falling short of its duty to teach the people to love their fellow men.

It is like watching a moth beat itself incessantly against a light. The point is never clarified, only turned around and around in obvious ways. It is clear that, if the writer opens each paragraph with such simple variations on his opening proposition, nothing is going on within the paragraph to make him see where he might take his point and develop it; when he gets to the end of each paragraph, he is still right back where he started.

To put the matter in more constructive terms, the writer does not ask himself how he sees something in relation to something else. The church is only a mirror of the ills of the society, not an antidote to them—that is the point, presumably, but the writer never sees this clearly enough to make it so. If he had, maybe he could then see that the racial problem is only a variation or a type of this main point, and if he had seen that, he might have seen that one of the main facts about Baldwin's essay is that it is not primarily about blacks and whites but about blindness and fear and about the church as a mask for these feelings. The writer does not ask himself what he is saying. In the second paragraph he quotes Baldwin to the effect that the principles underlying the church are "blindness, loneliness, and terror." But this really is too much for him; he seems to repeat the statement as a means of not facing it. He does not, as Baldwin does, see these words as expressing human feelings, but only as marking human failure.

If there is a place, therefore, where the paper loses its chance to develop, it is at the end of the second paragraph. Having quoted Baldwin on the principles underlying the church, having failed to note the sympathy and generosity with which Baldwin treats all sinners, the writer berates churchgoers: " 'Love thy neighbor' meant 'Love only those who belong to this church.' " This sentence, one notes, does not describe what Baldwin found at all. For, indeed the people in his church do not love each other. But having said this, the writer can move into position his big empty guns and, for two paragraphs, attack churchgoers for their hypocrisy in simple and obvious ways familiar to all of us: the church doesn't work; people evade its stated commandments; whites continue to hate blacks; and so on. The writer, having deflected from the complex tones of Baldwin's writing, enters into the never-never land of easy explanation. Once there, he sees no need to get out.

One way of saying what is wrong is that the writer does not read well. That is true enough, but is probably not a remark that can be of much help to the writer. It might be better to say that blindness, loneliness, and terror seem too strong feelings for him to face, so he translates them to mean "hypocrisy," which he, of course, *can* face—notice that when he chronicles instances of blindness, loneliness, and terror in the fourth paragraph, they are all just variants of hypocrisy. No comment of a teacher, no matter how beautifully and carefully phrased, could make this writer face up to blindness, loneliness, and terror, but it might help him to say that the paper becomes organizationally repetitious and incoherent when he doesn't face the implications of the material he begins to bring out in the second paragraph. He might at least be made to realize that Baldwin does ask him to see more than he is willing or able to see.

It is important to add, however, that the second paper allows a reader to say all this, whereas the first keeps itself hidden behind its truisms so as to make it almost invulnerable to sensitive attack. The failure of nerve, if that is in fact what it is, is so complete in the author of the first paper that there is no place one can point to and say: "Here is where you deflect from your point." With the second paper, though, such an identification is possible. Because the point of deflection comes early, most of the paper is worthless, or just about. But that fact itself is instructive, for it enables us to formulate a tidy little rule: the later the point in the paper where repetition takes over potential development, the better the paper. All papers, we can safely say, give out before the end, but those which really seek ways of expanding and exploring their subject keep open, keep developing for most of their length.

—*III*—

The Avenue in Harlem is full of pimps, whores, and racketeers, and this is not an atmosphere that can possibly help men to achieve their goal of coming closer to God. In *The Fire Next Time*, James Baldwin describes himself as a small boy fleeing from the wages of sin visible on the Avenue and going into the church, which, though ostensibly so far removed, is very much like the Avenue. On the surface it fights the spiritual damage of the Avenue, but, in fact, the church cooperates, does what the pimps and whores did.

Baldwin says that every Negro boy in his position looks for a gimmick to start him on his way. Baldwin's gimmick was the church, just as the gimmicks of so many others were the rackets and the vices found on the Avenue. Baldwin meets a woman whose question to him is "Whose little boy are you?," which is the same phrase used by the racketeers on the Avenue. By including this phrase in his essay Baldwin is saying that the church, too, is a racket. He admits it was just good luck that he found himself in the church racket rather than some other.

The church, the fortress against sin, uses sinful methods to bring people to its standard. It promotes their blindness so it can use their terror and loneliness to keep the people from leaving either the church or the Avenue. Both church and Avenue try to provide ways to relieve the peoples' loneliness so they will keep coming back. The church provides God, and the Avenue provides women or gambling or liquor. Both church and Avenue try to terrorize the people: the fear of being eternally damned against the fear of physical punishment and deprivation.

The church, according to Baldwin, is run on the same principle as the rackets: get as much money as you can from the customers. Ministers eventually acquire houses and Cadillacs while the congregations scrub floors. The church is the best business, and it has its people wear masks of love to hide their self-contempt and despair. Like the rackets, the church feels no responsibility for its customers after they leave the door. When the congregation leaves the building, religion leaves the congregation.

Religion is not fighting the rackets on the Avenue, because it is a part of them. All it does is to compete with the other powers for the business of the people of Harlem. The church is nothing for some, salvation for others, but it does not matter, because the church is a racket just like the Avenue.

It would be easy enough to show how this paper is much like the second one: just count the number of times it repeats its central proposition that the church is only another ghetto racket. I count eight sentences given over to these repetitions, at least a third of the paper.

Furthermore, it has a fault of its own, a tendency toward leaky paragraphs, where the sentences are only vaguely or partially related one to another: "Baldwin's gimmick was the church, just as the gimmicks of so many others were the rackets and vices found on the Avenue." That sentence points us in the direction of Baldwin's experiences in the church. But the next one pulls us back to the oft-repeated thesis: "Baldwin meets a woman whose question to him is 'Whose little boy are you?,' which is the same phrase used by the racketeers on the Avenue. By including this phrase in his essay Baldwin is saying that the church, too, is a racket." What's happened is that the sentences have been put in the wrong sequential order. Baldwin does not get the church as his gimmick until after he meets the lady preacher, and the point about that meeting is not just to say that the church is a racket, but to show that the boy was spiritually seduced beginning with the lady's smile; the phrase "Whose little boy are you?" implies much more than the racketeering of its speaker. But the writer, by putting Baldwin's experiences out of order, then by repeating his opening thesis, takes himself away from trying to show what Baldwin shows. Thus, the last sentence of the paragraph, though about a sentence embedded in Baldwin's paragraph about the preacher, is, in the writer's handling, cut off, and simply dangles: "He admits it was just good luck that he found himself in the church racket rather than some other."

The point may seem minor because it involves matters of small details and is obviously not crucial to any final judgment of the paper. But look what might happen if the sentences in this paragraph are little more than rearranged:

> Baldwin says every Negro in his position is forced to look for a gimmick to start him on his way. The summer he was fourteen, Baldwin stumbled on what was to become his gimmick when he met a lady preacher who asked him the same question the pimps and the racketeers were asking: "Whose little boy are you?" Because "I unquestionably wanted to be *somebody's* little boy . . . my heart replied at once, 'Why, yours.'" Baldwin admits it was just good luck that he found himself in the church racket rather than some other.

My paragraph is somewhat shorter than the original, but it moves its sentences along a path parallel to Baldwin's experience. In itself this helps create a smoothness in the motion of the sentences. But more important than that, it points toward a place to go next, and so shapes more than the one paragraph. Notice that in the original paper the writer, having just dropped his sentences on the page, is reduced to another restatement of the main thesis at the beginning of the next paragraph, almost to remind himself where he is. When a paragraph is as loose as the original one above, the writer's sense of direction gets lost, and it turns out that more is at stake than a few ill-organized sentences.

Still, this seems to me a somewhat better paper than the second one, though mostly for what might be done with it. In the first place, the writer, by treating Harlem as though it were just a place and not a ghetto, achieves the negative virtue of avoiding the junky talk about prejudice and bad white folk that most people feel compelled to write if they are white and their subject is black. One can not do full justice to Harlem or Baldwin by making them color-less, as it were, but one can say a lot of things that way, and also avoid saying a lot of other things. In the second place, this paper is about Baldwin's experience rather than about the moral rectitude of the author, and it tries to make its details offer a genuine sense of Baldwin's details. For instance, in the third paragraph, this writer says more about the way the ghetto church works than does the writer of the second paper, because he compares the church to the Avenue rather than to what it should be, though even this doesn't get the writing very close to Baldwin's magnificent descriptions of his experiences of exhilaration in the church. This paper places the phrase about the mask of love to hide self-hatred in a context where the phrase has much more meaning than it does in the second paper; here it is clear that the mask of love is not worn just so preachers can be hypocrites, but so they can be rich.

Further praise of this paper would be most unwise. It just isn't that good or that much different from the second. But its more sensitive use of details does show up the way the repetition is merely repetition; if you take out the sentences which state the thesis you are left with a rather lovely mess of details just crying out for an organization they do not have. Again the trouble seems to be that the writer has not asked himself where he might go with his proposition, what he might make of it, how he might take the word "racket" as applied to the church and go to work on Baldwin's description of the fervor and the hollowness of that fervor he experienced while part of that "racket." Instead, as far as this writer is concerned, Baldwin's essay is really over when it, in fact, is only a third of its final length; he settles for the comparison between church and Avenue, while Baldwin begins with that and keeps moving into the church, into his experience as a preacher, and out again on the other side. Baldwin develops, but the paper about him only repeats, and now we can take a closer look at Baldwin to see what the writers of these three papers miss.

Look at the two paragraphs that begin, "The church was very exciting." That sentence alone, by the way, is enough to expose the simplicity of the papers we have been considering. Without for a moment ignoring the blindness, self-hatred, and despair on which he has shown the church is based, Baldwin takes those very qualities and shows how they can be transformed into "excitement," "drama," "pathos," "triumphant and transfigured faces," and the "miracle" of "carrying the Word." The excitement and the transfiguration, of course, come from the theatricality of the church, even from the hypocrisy which accepts the drama of despair and joy as the truth about life. The church, with Baldwin as a member and leader of it, creates a community of anguish and rejoicing "in spite of—or, not inconceivably, because of—the shabbiness of my motives."

That idea is not a difficult idea to grasp, and no student is totally innocent of an experience in his own life where more than one feeling was expressed simultaneously or where the precise nature of one's motives was really irrelevant. Any child who has come to learn the depression of the day after Christmas knows that we often embrace excitement because it falsifies as well as heightens our normal sense of life. Anyone not totally committed to a sour view of life, furthermore, knows that such embracing is not adequately defined by calling it false or wicked. But Baldwin is far from finished: "I rushed home from school, to the church, to the altar, to be alone there, to commune with Jesus, my dearest Friend, who would never fail me, who knew all the secrets of my heart." Those last three phrases presumably are the phrases Baldwin used as he communed with Jesus down at the cross; the perspective is that of the fourteen-year old. In the next sentence the perspective shifts suddenly to that of the adult Baldwin: "Perhaps He did, but I didn't, and the bargain we struck, actually, down there at the foot of the cross, was that He would never let me find out." The shift indicates fully the shabbiness of the boy's motives, but does not for a moment remove the sympathy Baldwin has for his adolescent self. Jesus is being used shamelessly. The language that says the boy is being open and sincere in fact is employed to keep the boy from having to be open and sincere, but the sting of these truths does not turn the man Baldwin away from the boy Baldwin. To expose something is not the same thing as ridiculing or disparaging it.

Nor is Baldwin finished yet: "He failed His bargain. He was a much better Man than I took Him for. It happened, as things do, imperceptibly, in many ways at once." Notice that Baldwin does not, nor does he have to, declare himself a believer or an unbeliever in Jesus, and thereby he avoids any statement of belief that would falsely clear everything up. Jesus failed the boy by not keeping the bargain the boy had made with him, by not letting the boy's hypocrisy remain hidden. Such a statement implies "belief," of course, a beautiful respect for the un-shabbiness of Jesus. But Jesus failed Baldwin, as the paragraph goes on to show, only because time passed; the drama of the church could not continue to blot out the rest of life forever. Baldwin reads Dostoevski and meets Jews in his school, thereby gaining perspectives which slowly expose the falsity of the bargain with Jesus.

One could go on in this vein, taking each sentence and paragraph as it comes and showing how each one adds and modifies what has preceded; I have written two pages about only a few of Baldwin's sentences, and left a good deal out, too. Writing like this example from Baldwin's work can be talked about in many ways, and the closer one comes to it the less simple it becomes.

Yet, and here I feel insistent, writing like this is not beyond the comprehension of most students. What Baldwin is writing about becomes very complex, but not in ways that need startle anyone who has himself reached adolescence. For, of course, it is not Baldwin's experience by itself that is extraordinary but his way of being very critical and very generous toward his experience. The great and wonderful challenge of a writer like Baldwin is that he seems to show how much can be made of relatively simple experiences, and that challenge can be met in many ways, one of which is to see how much can be said by writing about his writing.

Having made these comments on Baldwin's essay as an example of what I mean by development rather than repetition, I would like to compare Baldwin's "paper" with a fourth example.

—IV—

The first shipment of Negroes to be sold as slaves arrived in this country in 1619; since then the Negro has been cruelly mistreated. Many white Americans are shocked by recent events concerning the Negro, mainly riots and the stubborn cry of "Black Power." Yet white America refuses to accept the Negro as an equal, and it has made this destruction necessary.

Before the Civil War Negroes were bought, sold, and traded because they were the property of their owners, who could and did treat them like cattle. The Thirteenth Amendment, passed just after the Civil War, declared that the Negro was free and equal to the white man. Yet he has never been treated as such. Society has been strictly segregated, from churches and schools to buses and drinking fountains. By supporting, enforcing, and simply living in this segregated society, the white man has held the Negro in a kind of slavery for the last hundred years.

James Baldwin shows how our treatment of the Negro has made him do the very things that shock and horrify us. Baldwin says, for example, "Negroes in this country . . . are taught really to despise themselves from the moment their eyes open on the world. The world is white and they are black." Why, then, are we surprised when Negro rioters loot, kill, and burn our major cities? If the Negro cannot respect himself, how can he respect the white man or the world the white man has created?

Many white people are alarmed and some are frightened by the Negroes' demand for black power. We have forgotten the power that held the Negro in servitude in America for 250 years, the white power: fear. The Negro today has realized the effect of the use of fear as a weapon; we are merely being served some of our own medicine.

We have been telling ourselves that Negroes are basically inferior for so long that we have begun to believe it; we felt secure in our superior position to the Negro. Now we feel insulted and a little afraid. The Negro has put one over on us; he has shown us what hypocrites we are.

The Negro is tired of his subordinate position. He has had his fill of segregation and discrimination. He wants only to be treated as an equal in a country that was founded on the doctrine of equality. And we have no right to deny them this equality.

If I were making comments on this paper, I would have few objections to make about its details. It is consistently fluent and coherent. It is, on almost all the usual grounds, superior to any of the first three papers, and if I have introduced a discussion of Baldwin himself to diminish this paper by comparison, if I want to object to this paper, I must first say that this writer has done well what most writers of composition are asked to do. The little rule formulated while discussing the second paper—the later repetitions begin, the better the paper—shows this easily enough. The next-to-last paragraph sputters and only repeats the one before it; at that point the writer can go no further, and the last paragraph summarizes and adds nothing. But the writer has gotten three-quarters of the way through his paper before the breakdown takes place.

It is a bulletproof paper, then, except for the closing paragraphs. In a world where the primary job of the student is to keep the teacher off his back, this student wins the game. But a bulletproof paper is still in the same league as the first three papers considered. It still sees writing as a task, sees paragraphs and sentences as vessels to be filled, sees intelligent competence as the highest possible achievement. It develops a point of view, but it does so along fairly easy lines and avoids all complexity.

We have considered this kind of paper before, in the preceding chapter; this paper is a superb instance of the arguable proposition. But here I would like to come at the matter a little differently and say that the development of this paper is made orderly for most of its length by confining itself within strict limits. The first two paragraphs are not, strictly speaking, mere throat-clearing; they do say something. But notice how they talk about "the Negro" in simple ways; "the Negro" is a class of being. Such a term is perhaps satisfactory enough when considering such matters as slavery and the Thirteenth Amendment, because slavery and the Thirteenth Amendment consider the Negro as a class of being too. But in the third paragraph the writer comes to Baldwin, where the consideration is not broadly political but psychological: ". . . our treatment of the Negro has motivated him to do the very things that shock and horrify us." As a simple statement this is probably true enough, but at this point such a simple statement is really concealing almost as much, if not more, than it is revealing.

The writer looks to Baldwin for support, properly, and so should we. He finds a statement in Baldwin about psychology that is broad and encompassing, and so he quotes it. But Baldwin's essay and the writer's paper meet at a point where the writer is being his most specific and Baldwin is being his most general. Or, to put it another way, the fact that "the world is white and they are black" is a fact which can, as Baldwin abundantly shows, lead to a whole variety of responses among black people. Baldwin himself responds differently at different times, and each time in a different way from the way of his father, the lady preacher, and the racketeers on the Avenue. Behind Baldwin's generalization is a world of people, each responding to the same general truth, but each responding differently. In the writer's version of the same general truth, however, this variety disappears, and we have only means of "understanding" rioters and looters. The psychology the writer describes makes sense enough—as long as we ignore Baldwin. He has, in effect, moved into the rich and varied world Baldwin describes and taken from it only that which most easily fits his sense of Negro psychology. Because what the writer takes from Baldwin is there for the taking, and because what the writer says is true enough, his paper is the best of the four we have considered. But the truth of his proposition about Negro psychology is a thin truth, arguable certainly, but thin, and in the face of Baldwin, almost inhuman in that thinness. Compare two sentences:

> If the Negro cannot respect himself, how can he respect the white man or the world the white man has created?

> I remember, anyway, church suppers and outings, and, later, after I left the church, rent and waistline parties where rage and sorrow sat in the darkness and did not stir, and we ate and drank and talked and laughed and forgot all about "the man."

"If the Negro cannot respect himself, how can he respect the white man or the world the white man has created?"—all true. But looking at the second sentence we see a largeness and complexity of human response that almost repudiates the simple truth. The writer, to put it another way, simply could not quote Baldwin's sentence without destroying the even, simple machinery he has established. As a white person, the writer cannot be expected to know anything like what Baldwin knows about what it is like to be black. But he can read, Baldwin writes in English, and if he can do that he can begin to realize that his sense of Negro psychology is in its infancy because he lets his sense of human beings remain so infantile.

These last words are harsh, but the writer of this paper can take it. The world as presently constructed should be pretty much his oyster, and he almost certainly is intelligent enough to know that he would not develop an argument about himself along the same simplistic lines that he develops his sense of Negro psychology. The last thing he wants is to be patronizing to his subject, but inevitably, when a complex subject is treated simplistically, some condescension is the result. The trouble does not lie, I am convinced, in the moral character of the writer, but in his needlessly embattled sense of the world, school, and what it takes to write. The whole tone of the paper is one that implies a rather simple-minded audience that has not read Baldwin and has only bigots as sources of information. As a result, the paper has an antiseptic quality to it—untouched by human hands, as it were—that stands, if nothing else, in striking contrast to the manner of Baldwin's essay, with its sense of a determined exploration of human complexity.

To develop an argument is to essay one's mind, to try something out, to push as far as one can. It is to recognize that one can know what one knows and with great security and yet, in relation to what the subject offers, know not very much. So the mind moves out, constantly examining the relation of one thing to another, constantly asking, "If this, then what?" The task is never to "cover" a subject, for that task can safely be left to others. It is, rather, to find out what one thinks. If you know just what you think before you start, inevitably the antiseptic quality creeps in, the mind goes slack, and repetition is the result. To repeat is to stop, to develop is to go on. As long as one commits oneself to this idea of going on, good writing is possible; the moment one stops, competent writing is all one can hope for.

4

STYLE, USAGE,
AND GRAMMAR

Style is as style does, or, style that works is good. Some writers can be eloquent with short, choppy sentences filled with monosyllables, others can make long and labyrinthine sentences clear and apparently simple. The only obvious rule about style is that it is seldom good when it becomes a game of special effects and is usually good when it is easily and apparently naturally arrived at. Often it takes years of effort to achieve a style so naturally one's own that it really does come easily, and most of the advice given writers about style tends to lead them to work on special effects. As a result, little in this chapter will concern itself with style as such. At the beginning I want to talk about how the context of English courses affects the style and tone of many students, and then address the difficult problem of jargon and its effects on style and tone.

The Style of English Papers

The great fault of the style of most students is its tendency toward stiffness, solemnity, and pompousness. Students apparently are told that they should be forceful, unblinking, and forever mindful that an English paper is a formal occasion. One result is the use of a great many words that would never be used on lesser occasions, another is a tone that tends to imply the reader is something of a fool. Here is a list to show the kinds of words and phrases I mean: due to, occurrence, striking difference, unadulterated, the latter, the former, as is evidenced by, individual (used to refer to a person), unique, effective, clarify, assess, reassess, to the fullest, more or less, benefit (especially when used as a verb), the young, the aged or the elderly, essential, fundamental, viewpoint, statement, unusual, faced with, in the face of, technique, symbolic, climax (especially when used as a verb). Most of these words have their good use at one time or another, and the point about them is not that they should not be used but that they bespeak a fairly narrow range of manner within which almost all English papers, unfortunately, are written. The corresponding tone is something like this:

> Do Americans today regard religion as a sacred institution or as a convenient escape mechanism fom the pressures and frustrations of life? The latter seems to be the more prevalent view, as religion is used to dissipate fears and to provide a blanket of security to shut out the chill winds of reality. Love of God and His wonders is secondary to cowering before Him in hopes of not offending Him and therefore gaining easy admittance to heaven.

"The latter seems to be the more prevalent view . . ." Why should anyone ever write a phrase like that, or like "therefore gaining easy admittance to heaven"? Whom is this writer speaking to? Why?

Most classrooms for most students are alien territory, where the language spoken ranges from one slightly different from their common speech to one downright foreign, and a good student sees he will get along better if he adopts the teacher's language. In addition, many English teachers, when they come to speak of written style, emphasize "rhetoric," by which they mean style as a matter of occasion, situation, and audience. In fact, of course, students write for their teachers, but instead of accepting that obvious truth, teachers often ask students to speak to an audience of unknown thousands. When students write for an audience which both student and teacher know does not exist, they often feel that their writing is something foreign to them. When the nonexistent audience is one that seems to require stiffness and solemnity from the writer, the result is even worse.

Now occasion, situation, and audience can be important considerations for a writer, but when they are allowed to override all others, silliness is usually the result, as happens when intelligent and well-meaning people, sixteen to twenty-two years old, feel obliged to speak as though delivering the Gettysburg Address. Most people do not have difficulty speaking to their audience if they are simply left on their own. They do not speak to an elderly, dignified stranger as they do to kids down the street, and they do not naturally write love letters in the style they use in a letter of application. Someone whose usual vocabulary when speaking with contemporaries is a combination of words like "weirdo," "fantastic," "groovy," "shit," "hey," "boss," "what's happening?," "marvy," and "neat" rightly feels that these words won't quite do when he is a student addressing his teacher. This does not mean, however, that he is duty-bound to fill his speech or his writing with "due to the fact that" and "on the contrary" and "to the fullest extent" and all the rest.

Ideally one's style will not shift much to suit different situations; it will not in conversation be a series of grunts, whoops, and profanities, and it will not in writing be much different from one's speech. A style that is truly portable is a style that will be expressive of the person using it. Most people know this and admire those who speak and write in roughly the same way. Students generally do not like teachers, for instance, who try to adopt the current slang of students any more than they like teachers who speak as though they were in a museum or a tomb. All good style is dignified because it does express the speaker with an integrity any audience must respect. Yet, because most teachers have not achieved such a style, and because classrooms, assignments, and textbooks are the context of teachers far more than they are the context of students, most students grow up convinced that their style, especially in their written work, should

[129]

not aim to be expressive of the person but should aim to be satisfactory to the audience. Good students achieve this mediocre goal, bad students do not, but both aim at the same unsatisfactory achievement, and are encouraged to do so.

A simple example. Any teacher and most students know that some of the finest speaking they have ever heard comes in a really good class discussion, a discussion that, for some mysterious reason, stops being filled with ploys and attitudinizing and seems, for a little while, to express the emphases and urgencies the students truly feel. On the one hand, the style is better than that usually used by students among themselves, because the presence of the teacher and the organized circumstances of the classroom force students to avoid their usual slackness and to complete their thoughts, to choose their words with whatever care can be mustered. On the other hand, the language does not have the stiffness and the awful mixture of hesitancy and pompousness that are the usual result of the students' awareness that they are students and speaking to a teacher. At such a moment, speech is still speech, but it does not have the conversational vices that encourage us to substitute vague personal good will for precision of language. These moments are rare, yet everyone has known and been excited by them. They cannot, of course, be self-consciously achieved or repeated, but I have often felt that if we could acknowledge such moments as an ideal of style, everyone's writing would improve.

The Nature of Jargon

My dictionary defines "jargon" in a way that begins to identify the problem and to show why it is *the* great problem about style in the world of English papers now. Jargon is:

1. the language peculiar to a particular trade, profession, or group: medical jargon; plumbers' jargon.
2. unintelligible or meaningless talk or writing; gibberish.
3. any talk or writing which one does not understand.

On the one hand jargon is technical language, and on the other it is meaningless language. It is not hard to see how the word came to have both meanings. Jargon is a language which can be used precisely by those within the trade, profession, or other group who know what the words mean, and it is also an abuse of language when the same words are used imprecisely or wrongly by those not within the trade, profession, or group, and who do not know and seldom seriously ask what the words mean. The American student, from first grade through doctoral research, is surrounded by jargons, many of which he probably finds confusing, funny, impressive, or threatening. Of all the areas that are expanding at accelerating rates in this country, the technical languages are expanding fastest, and the school system is where these languages collide with each other and with people not yet adept in their usage. To be a good student is to master various jargons; to be a bad student is to wander in a world that now resembles a maze, now resembles a jungle.

It was not always thus, and perhaps a little history can show why the problem is so acute today. In the middle of the eighteenth century Samuel Johnson compiled the first important English dictionary, and at the time he was aware that the language was expanding beyond the capacity of any one man to keep abreast of it. New terms were coming into the language via business, trade, and the professions; Johnson's word for their languages was "cant." At the same time, Henry Fielding, in his novels *Joseph Andrews* and *Tom Jones*, was satirizing people, mostly professionals, who used cant phrases or jargon to intimidate and defraud others. Lawyers, doctors, and ministers were his favorite targets, but a lady who is trying to seduce a young man, and who constantly refers to her "virtue," "honor," and "chastity" gets into the act, too. For both Johnson and Fielding, the language is capable of being used with precision and beauty only if it is free of cant; what we might call the common language is not only sufficient for the speech and writing of the common man but is essential. Johnson's dictionary works by deriving its meanings from quotations of poets and philosophers; for him their language is his language, as the technical language of a banker or a diplomat or a blacksmith is not, and his language is the language of all men who read and write. Johnson believed that the best interests of the language could be served by keeping its jargons separate from the rest and foresaw what would happen when jargon and cant terms came into the common language.

A great deal happened to the language in the next 150 years, but if we compare Johnson's *Dictionary of the English Language* with H. W. Fowler's *Dictionary of Modern English Usage* (1926), we will probably feel that both works are products of an age long past. Fowler, like Johnson, feels obliged to be on his guard against incursions into the language by people or groups who did not really know what they were doing. If, for Johnson, most cant was spoken and written by working people in their working world, for Fowler "the enemy" was mostly writers in newspapers and magazines, and to him their insensitivity to grammar and common sense was at least as serious as their use of cant terms or jargon. Furthermore, the current crises in the language all come from sources that alarmed Fowler no more than they did Johnson, perhaps not even as much. Fowler has a section he calls "Popularized Technicalities," in which he lists words that have crept into common usage after having been originally coined as technical terms. Understandably, he insists that most popularized technical terms often very badly misrepresent the original meaning, which is true enough, but his list of terms shows words so much in common use today that often it is hard to remember they were once part of a special language: category, asset, complex (as a noun), implicit, dilemma, flamboyant, concept, dualistic, intensive, decimate, chronic. As I and perhaps most people look at that list of "technical terms," I wonder if I commonly misrepresent their original meaning. If, in 1926, "implicit" or "dilemma" were technical terms liable to popular abuse, they are not that, or simply that, any longer.

We have been bringing jargon into the language for a long time now, and it ill behooves anyone to object to popular use of a given word simply on the puristic grounds that a technical term should be used only by those who understand its technical meaning. Two related things have happened, however, since Fowler's time, to challenge the idea that the language is the language and there's nothing that can be done about it. First, in the past fifty years, there has been a vast increase in the number of areas of study, each one of which has felt obliged to institute and even to sanctify its own jargon. What are now called the social sciences—history, political science, economics, anthropology, sociology, psychology, social work, and the various hybrids thereof—have all grown greatly, become compartmentalized and specialized, and therefore been subject to the pressure to develop their own languages. In addition, the number and kinds of natural sciences have increased greatly. A number of older occupations—nursing, coaching, fishing, foresting, farming—have all become more organized into professions and areas of research. Public servants from police, firemen, and prison authorities to specialists in public administration have felt the influence of a growing bureaucratic and technological pressure to categorize and specialize their languages: a cop is an officer, his tickets are citations, and he has to have at least some knowledge of criminology, penal theory, social work, and the law—each with its own language—just in order to be a cop who can give you a ticket. Samuel Johnson could make, and without difficulty defend the idea of, a dictionary of common language; dictionary makers today must work in teams and committees just to begin to keep up with the vast expansion of jargons. If you look down a page of an ordinary modern dictionary, you will find that at least half the words are part of one technical language or another.

But the second thing to happen, which is only an outgrowth or development of the first, is really what must concern us, and that is that the American student is now being told and is learning very quickly that his success or even survival in school is dependent on his ability to learn jargons. He speaks whatever it is that is the common language, but he knows that this language, in many instances, simply is of no use to him as he moves along in school. He may learn French or Spanish as a foreign language, but so too must he learn language arts, social studies, physical science, and even in elementary school he will also run into economics, psychology, and physical education, and in most cases these too are foreign languages. He may, in his French class, be asked to "Traducez en Français" and he may feel it is

[133]

fair enough for a French teacher to want to speak to him and ask him questions in French, so he may come to use the language as though it were not foreign. But when he goes to his next class, what is he to make of a test that gives him a list of things and asks him to "reduplicate matching pairs"? That is not a foreign language, perhaps, but it shares with French a great foreignness from the student's everyday speech, and it also shares with French the fact that it is a language he only encounters once a day, in this class. By the time most students reach college they are so accustomed to the fact of jargons that they are often upset, confused, and angry when asked to speak or write without a jargon. Indeed, why should a student think that he ought to make his own writing make sense when he must spend most of his time "translating" various jargons into English before he can understand them?

Listen:

In this section I have developed a critical vocabulary that will enable the student to see the work of literature more completely.

That sentence is audacious and foolish, but so common that few notice. It presumes that if someone wants to "see" a work of literature what he needs is a jargon, a "critical vocabulary." At best this assertion is mistaken, at worst it is almost criminal. The poor student is told about narrators and pseudonarrators, about symbolic and normative functions, about myths and archetypes, about phenomenological aspects and representational elements, about distancing effects, narrative and dramatic ironies, about seven types of ambiguity and four stages of Renaissance style and the many kinds of "comoedic adjustments that insure societal continuations," and then is told that if he "learns" all this he will be able to "see" one, several, or all works of literature. Of course, in fact, all he has is a weighty and unhelpful vocabulary with which to describe whatever he sees, and probably the nagging suspicion that he could describe whatever he sees in much simpler and more precise terms. In the study of literature, however, the student has the advantage of having the literature to read, and it, at least, is not liable to seem like jargon, even though it may seem foreign. In the study of, say, sociology, the student has no alternative or palliative to the jargon. He begins his study of the subject with someone saying, in effect, "These are the terms we use here; learn them." In most cases, all a student is ever asked to do is define and use the jargon satisfactorily.

It seems to me that this is a potentially disastrous fact about the world that confronts the student, but nothing I can say is going to change it. There is no point in my advising anyone not to use jargon when jargon can, indeed, be used well. Rather, what I would like to do is try to make some distinctions about the language and the impact of so many jargons on it. The motto is this: even jargons can be made to make sense, and we can all think sensibly about the matter.

Let us start with some examples. First, "relate" and "inter-relate." In *Modern English Usage* Fowler makes some very nice and careful distinctions between "relation" and "relationship," but we now use the two words interchangeably, though I notice "relationship" is becoming the more popular of the two, presumably because it is the longer. There would be no point in my rehearsing Fowler, because "relation" and "relationship" are now the same word and that is that. The impulse to make all words longer, though, has led to the invention of a word Fowler had probably never heard of: "interrelate." I call it a word, and I note its presence in my dictionary, but it has no reason for existing because "interrelate" means, quite simply, "relate." In some cases "interrelate" is so common that it sounds better than "relate," but in no case does it mean anything different or more precise. My dictionary seems to have been compiled by those who know this, but who also know their clients will expect "interrelate" in the dictionary, so they proceed to make matters worse by defining "interrelate" as "reciprocally related." And you know what "reciprocally related" means: "related." An example. Geographically the United States and Canada are "related" and the relation is "reciprocal," because one can say the US is south of Canada or that Canada is north of the US. Perhaps you do not hear that the US and Canada are geographically "interrelated," but you might easily hear that their economies are "interrelated." It sounds plausible because such statements are common. But to say the economies of the

US and Canada are "interrelated" is to say only that in some way, as yet unspecified, they are "related."

This is no trivial matter, either, because, for some reason, people who say that "the economies of the United States and Canada are interrelated" almost always feel that "interrelate" says more than it does, and they never go on to describe the relatedness involved. The longer word casts a spell on its user, and when it does, incompleteness or vagueness is the result. Jargon is like that because the use of jargon is all too often a sign of status. Other words that seem to be both unnecessary and popular because they are longer and apparently more impressive sounding to their users are: societal (for social), analyzation (for analysis), structure (for build), finalize (for finish or do), position (for job), confront (for face), explore (for look or think), utilize (for use), indicate (for say), maximize or multiply (for increase). Here is one class of words that can, quite simply, be avoided. In some cases to do so is to be precise or accurate instead of vague; in all cases to do so is to begin to believe that to make sense, rather than impressive sounds, out of one's language is a step toward being civil and civilized.

A second example: "disinterested" and "uninterested." This is not, strictly speaking, a matter of jargon, though it is easily associated with jargon, because those who confuse "disinterested" and "uninterested" are apt to be those who talk about things being "interrelated" and who are impressed with the command to "reduplicate matching pairs." The important word here is "disinterested," because it does not really have a good synonym, so if it is misused an idea and a human possibility will pass out of our lives. To be "disinterested" is not to be "uninterested" or "indifferent"; those words imply lack of concern, boredom. Neither does it simply mean "objective" or "detached," though these words come much closer to defining it. To be "objective" or "detached" is to be personally uninvolved and therefore capable of unbiased judgments, and this much is true of being "disinterested." But whereas "objective" and "detached" imply a lack of feeling, "disinterested" does not. One can be passionately interested in a problem and still be able to examine it "disinterestedly"; indeed, this combination of deep concern and detachment is precisely the quality most needed, say, in a judge or for most research. To be unselfishly engaged, to care deeply but not for reasons of personal gain or well-being, is to be disinterested. If this meaning for "disinterested" effectively passes from the language, to be replaced on the one hand by "uninterested" and on the other by "detached," that will mean that the quality described by the word will no longer seem possible or desirable, and that will mean that somehow the world does not believe that one can care deeply but unselfishly.

Or, if that sounds too portentous, try "point of view" and "viewpoint." Here the question is not as strictly one of a meaning lost as of a metaphor blurred and so effectively lost. The idea behind "point of view" is that we do see things differently depending where we stand to look at them, so that your "point of view" and mine as we look at the same thing may be different, and if you ask me to see something from your "point of view," you are insisting that to do so will help me to see the object in question more completely. However, "point of view" has always seemed a little awkward to many people, mostly because, in practice, it usually involves a repetition of the word "of" ("from the point of view of . . ."), so "viewpoint" or its attendant, "standpoint," came into existence. When this happened the idea of a point from which one sees got lost, the idea that there are for most questions many points of view became obscured, and "viewpoint" became a synonym for "thinking" or "idea," as in "I'd like to get your viewpoint" or, even stranger, "I'd like to get your viewpoint*s*." In other words, if I ask you what your point of view is on a given subject, I should be asking you where you stand and what you see from where you stand; if I ask your viewpoint on a subject, I almost always have lost that sense of stance, of position, of a point from which the viewing takes place. In fact, "viewpoint" has become a synonym for "thought" and probably belongs in the class of words that includes "interrelate" and "finalize." "Point of view," however, like "disinterested," has a meaning that needs to be retained. What is distressing about these two examples is that, once a meaning has passed out of the language, it is almost impossible to get it back, and most people apparently grow up not knowing the meaning of the word "disinterested" or not seeing the metaphorical emphasis of "point of view," and so they blithely use "disinterested" to mean "uninterested" and "viewpoint" to mean "thought." At this point an individual by himself who is seeking to make sense cannot see what has gone wrong.

Perhaps the most striking and touching instance of a jargon that has seriously distorted a meaning and a possibility is the word "potential." The word originally was strictly an adjective, and except for some special uses in mathematics and physics, an adjective it should still be. It means "possible," "capable," or "latent," as opposed to some present actuality. If I say someone is a potential major league first baseman, I mean simply that that person could be, is capable of being, a major league first baseman. What happens, however, when "potential" becomes a noun is really disastrous. If I say someone has potential or is a person with potential, I am indicating . . . what? Notice that what before was a possibility for the future is now a fact in the present; but what kind of fact is it? To have potential is to have and yet not to have something never named; one has it because the verb is in the present tense, and one doesn't have it, because "potential" must describe a quality or fact not yet in existence.

Petty? Not at all. Some students are told by teachers and counselors and adults in general from the time they begin school that they have potential. But to have potential is not like having measles or fifty cents or the ability to hit a baseball; it is to have something you haven't. No one says potential actor, scientist, bully, or philosopher to thereby restore the word's status as an adjective. Instead, "potential" is allowed to stay a noun, vague and rather scary to most students who have "it." For the phrase is used as a whip—"You have this quality, but because you don't have it, you've got to work hard to get it"—and the student is not even treated as well as the beast of burden who at least is whipped in order to be told to move or move faster in a given direction. The whip stings, because "you have potential" implies that the person has not done something or is not yet what he should be, but it offers no direction, no answer to the question, "potential what?" In fact, it is the necessary word, the word that had insidiously to be invented to justify the batteries of tests given endlessly to students in this country that measure "ability" rather than "achievement." Give a test and then, if a student does well, he has "it," "potential," and that potential can haunt him and make him feel that somehow he is not what he should be. A couple of years ago I met a very nice young man who had, at some point in life, scored 134 on an IQ test, and that certainly meant he had potential. From that point onward he had been cajoled, flattered, hounded, scolded by everyone in power to live up to his potential. When I met him I made the same mistake, and I kept thinking that there must be some way to interest the boy into being what the test has said he could potentially be. But no, nothing I or his other teachers at the time could do could make him somehow equal that 134 IQ. During the time I knew him he fretted that fact a great deal and eventually began to do worse instead of better, and finally he dropped out of school altogether. No one had said to him, "You are a potential mathematician or engineer." Instead all they said was, "You are a potential x; that 134 says so," which is another way of saying, "Never mind who you are; think about what you could be, except I don't know what it is."

So, just as something valuable can be lost in the language and life when a word like "disinterested" loses its proper meaning, so can something quite sinister come into the language and life when a word gains a meaning it has no business having. I seldom get as nervous or frightened about what goes on in this country as I do when I start thinking about the potential uses for "potential" used as a noun.

Abuse of Parts of Speech

This discussion of "potential," while carrying us to the heart of the matter of jargon, also raises another problem, or another way of looking at the same problem concerning parts of speech, which demands at least some consideration by itself. In talking about parts of speech, I am mindful of some of the many things that have been happening in linguistics and grammar to change our ways of thinking about them, but for present purposes, the term "parts of speech" can mean what it means in the dictionary:

the classes of words which, taken together, form the whole language when seen grammatically.

Just as when dealing with jargons and their acceptance into the common language, so is it easy to fall into a kind of false purity about parts of speech. A moment's reflection shows that one of the best ways to keep the language alive is to have great flexibility both in the creation of new words and in the creation of new grammatical relations among existing words, and no sooner could rules on these matters be made to prevail than the language would become unuseful to its users. Misuse and flexibility are not the same thing. We easily and naturally start with one word and, by changing it or its grammatical relation, change its part of speech. "Enjoy" is a verb; "enjoyable" is an adjective; "enjoyment" is a noun; "enjoyably" is an adverb. "Horror" is a noun; "horrify" is a verb; "horrible" is an adjective; "horribly" is an adverb. "Exciting," "entertaining," and "diverting" are participles of verbs which we also use as adjectives; the same is true for past participles such as "murdered," "elected," and "completed." We need this way of tinkering with the language, and we need also to see what it can lead to.

It is, for instance, very easy to go haywire in deriving new words from old ones if the old word is not properly understood. At some time in this century the verb "to minimize" was derived from the noun "minimum." The verb is never an elegant one, and seldom does it seem a really necessary one. "Minimum" means "the least possible size, number, or amount," and so "minimize" means "decrease to the least possible amount." What happens, however, is that the word gets used to mean "reduce," as in "Leaving a light on when not at home considerably minimizes the risk of burglary." The sentence, as it stands, is nonsense because merely leaving a light on does not "decrease to the *least* possible amount" the chance of burglary. Another false use for "minimize" comes in a sentence like this: "It would be dangerously easy to minimize the effects of the earthquake," where the word means "underestimate." In both cases, when the sense of "minimum" as a superlative is lost, misuse of the verb is bound to result. In another case, the word "mobile" is made into "mobilize," which can have a perfectly legitimate meaning, "to put into motion," as in "The troops are being mobilized." The word is abused when the act of mobilizing could take place only if the thing mobilized were first transformed, as in "He mobilized public opinion"; you can't put public opinion into motion, though you can arouse the opinions of people so they will vote for you. In still other cases, words very hard to use correctly, like "dimension" or "concrete," get tossed about until they mean almost anything, at which point they are turned into adjectives like "dimensional" or verbs like "concretize" which don't stand a chance in the world of being used intelligibly.

One of the most frequently ridiculed but still popular changes of a part of speech is the addition of "wise" to make an adjective or adverb out of a noun: "Weatherwise, it looks bad, but moralewise everything is still in good shape." I think the origin of this usage, or at least the origin of its popularity, is advertising, and many English teachers feel they have said enough to discredit a usage if they say it is the invention of admen. The suffix "-wise" originally was the equivalent of the suffix "-ways" concerning some words like "slantways" or "slantwise," and in some other words "-wise" was established long ago: likewise, otherwise, clockwise. What happened, however, was that the suffix came to be used as a means of avoiding the natural or obvious subject. To say "Weatherwise, it looks bad" instead of "The forecast predicts rain" is to blur everything: who or what is *it?* how can "look" make sense or what is being looked at? Here the mistake might simply be classified as being awkward and needlessly obscure, and in most cases this is all that is wrong, though that is enough when simpler and more direct ways of expressing the same thought are always available. But read a few of these and see if you don't find the world they imply is very brutal, fuzzy, or irresponsible: "Girlwise, he was a smooth operator"; "Timewise, it doesn't matter"; "He has a very good thing, moneywise." Some things just shouldn't be put so simply into classes, and almost everything, if it is going to be put into a class, should be done so more carefully. As a footnote to this: People who seek to avoid the suffix "-wise" by means of the phrase "in terms of" are not doing themselves a favor. "In terms of weather, things look bad" is an absurdity. The phrase "in terms of" is like the phrase "point of view"—both are best used when their literal meaning is apparent to the speaker. The weather has no terms, though weather charts do, so to say "in terms of weather" is to ignore what "terms" means. Words, numbers, signs, all symbolic expressions are "terms"; things and abstract qualities are not; "in terms of" is properly used, then, only when terms are, in fact, involved.

In all these cases sense can prevail, and words badly or nonsensically coined or used seldom last in the language, or else they come to have meanings which are useful and expressive. To think about "avail" and "available," "indicate" and "indicative," "manifest" and "manifestly," and many other cases is to see that words indeed can be made of other words and eventually come to bear only partial witness to the word of their birth. We survived these nicely enough, and there is no reason to believe we cannot survive "minimize" used to mean "decrease," if indeed we must. "Quote" is now popularly used as a noun, though "quotation" is right there, and is even preferable; "human," too, is used as a noun, though "human being" is still considered correct. As long as we really do know and can say what we mean, we need neither fear nor be purists.

Another, and at least equally dangerous, abuse of parts of speech is the result of nouns indiscriminately used as adjectives. It is rather fun to make verbs out of nouns and adjectives, and the effect can be quite striking; Shakespeare's Cleopatra says of one who is hypocritically negotiating with her, "He words me, girls, he words me," and when she imagines a boy acting her part she says she fears he will "boy my greatness." "I'll fierce you" has always seemed to me a potentially useful phrase, and verbs like "to greeting" and "to introduction" are nice to use when you want to show the introducing or greeting was more formal or automatic than it might have been. But using nouns as adjectives is another matter, because it establishes, or seeks to establish, relations among words not normally capable of being related.

We speak and write without hesitation of "the football player," "the college student," and "the beauty parlor," and thereby make adjectives out of nouns. There may be something awkward about the phrases, but they certainly are not inferior to adjectives like "collegiate" and "sartorial," which seem invented primarily to avoid the awkwardness. But consider the following phrases: happiness curve, frustration quotient, friendship grouping, population explosion, salvation oriented, kinship taboos; and then ask what relation these nouns-as-adjectives have to the nouns they are intended to modify. For instance, in order for there to be a happiness curve, happiness must be in some statistical way measurable, and people must be able to say they are ecstatic, very happy, satisfied, able to live with, unsatisfied, or miserable. If the happiness one is measuring is, say, one's feelings about a new car or insurance agent, then it should be possible to check an appropriate box on a questionnaire so someone can make a happiness curve. But to think that one's feelings about one's wife or one's life can be expressed by checking a box in a questionnaire is to be, quite simply, brutal, and people who ask other people to do this are both fools and knaves. Wives are not cars, happiness does not belong on curves. Likewise, a world that has known the explosion of the populations of Hiroshima and Nagasaki should be able to find a better way of expressing its sense that the birth rate is rising much faster than the death rate than the term "population explosion." People who care about such things as friendship and salvation know that what matters most about them cannot be grouped or oriented (notice, by the way, that people were so pleased with a nice, vague and impressive sounding word like "orient" that they had to invent the redundant "orientate"). Something important is at stake—happiness, friendship, birth and death, salvation—and in each case it is being yoked violently to another noun and left as a matter merely to be measured and classified.

But more deep-rooted than this is the vagueness and sloppiness that almost inevitably attend the frequent use of nouns as adjectives. A "dream world," for instance, can be a world in which one dreams or the world one has always dreamed about; an "image conscious" person, given the current and most popular use of "image," is not someone who is conscious that he sees images but who may be conscious of his own image, of other peoples' images, or merely of public relations (notice, too, that "conscious" is not really very clear when used this way). The "dog leash law" would seem to be a law about dog leashes, though one presumes it is intended to be a law about dogs. "A status position" can be lots of things, among them "a position which confers a desirable status," where "position" means "job" and "status" means "good," or a "position where status can be assigned," where "position" means "someplace recognizable" and "status" means "class." In all these cases, at least one of the words is being used in ways that torture it, so that the reader or listener just has to hope he knows what the person is talking about because the person himself obviously does not, probably does not know he does not know, and may not even care. This kind of usage is the almost inevitable result of a world getting more and more full of jargons spoken by people who never asked, and were never urged to ask, about how things relate to each other. When adjectives do not really modify nouns but instead are themselves nouns jammed against other nouns, then relations are not clear; jargon is difficult enough to learn to use well without its effects also being felt in collapsed or decrepit grammar.

At this point I would like to try to summarize the argument before moving on to talk about cliches. The style of most students is under the very heavy pressure of jargons derived from the many professions and disciplines that operate within the school system, and the proper task of the student is neither to master the jargons nor to abjure them completely but to try at all times to see what sense and nonsense his words make. The great temptation with jargons is to make them self-justifying by making them difficult and impressive, so that a beginner might feel that if he learns a jargon he has learned a subject. This temptation must at all costs be resisted. In many ways the mistake that can be made with jargons is like the mistake so often made about organization and outlines and for similar reasons. Many areas of study in the social sciences and the humanities have organized or outlined their fields by means of manipulating the technical terms that make up their jargon. Most introductory textbooks in, say, sociology begin by defining "sociology" and "anthropology" and "social psychology" and "political science" and go on to offer many theories, each with its own manipulation of these large definitions, about what sociology is or should be. The student who is introduced to sociology is introduced via definitions, via a special language, as though what distinguished a sociologist from someone else were not a method or a field of study but a jargon. To make matters worse, most sociologists are rather careless writers, so that their explanations of their jargon tend to entangle them in still more jargon rather than to show in more common language the usefulness of their special terms. What the student is then tempted to do is to master the language, whereas what he should be doing is to translate it so as to deprive the jargon of its false impressiveness and, very often, its false precision. Most of the time this translation may involve nothing more elaborate than saying "kinship taboos" are (in English, as it were) "taboos about kinship," and recognizing as the translation is made that "about" is not a very clear word here either, and so further translation may be desirable or necessary. Keeping oneself alert to this constant need for translation is like keeping oneself asking, moment-to-moment, what relations between words and phrases one really means.

Furthermore, it is the only way to avoid cliches, mixed, silly, and dead metaphors, and the other faults in writing that will be discussed next.

What Is a Cliche?

We begin with two examples:

During the few weeks of life now left to him by his Maker, David tried to pour into everything he did the passions of a lifetime. He worked feverishly and with unbounded energy, he enjoyed his wine, his women, and his songs to the fullest. Undaunted by his date with death, he perceived his life, liberty, and pursuit of happiness as though learning of them all for the first time. His infectious and unquenchable thirst for living gave birth to new hopes and vigor for all around him, especially for those who knew and loved him best. True to himself to the last, he became a living legend, a symbol of man's unconquerable will to be the master of his fate and the captain of his soul.

There appears to be a vast amount of confusion on this point, but I do not know many Negroes who are eager to be "accepted" by white people, still less to be loved by them; they, the blacks, simply don't wish to be beaten over the head by the whites every instant of our brief passage on this planet. White people will have quite enough to do in learning how to accept and love themselves and each other, and when they have achieved this— which will not be tomorrow and may very well be never—the Negro problem will no longer exist, for it will no longer be needed.

The second of these examples was written by James Baldwin, and is from the selection of *The Fire Next Time* printed in the preceding chapter. It is hard to say who wrote the first. I did, in the sense that that particular arrangement of these words has never been made before, though every phrase in it has been used a thousand times before.

As people are usually asked to think about cliches, the first example is filled with them and the second is not. Someone who collects trite or hackneyed phrases could take almost every word from the first for his catalogue: the few weeks left to him; left him by his Maker; the passions of a lifetime; worked feverishly; unbounded energy; wine, women, and song; undaunted; date with death; life, liberty, and the pursuit of happiness; infectious; unquenchable thirst; those who knew him best; those who loved him best; true to himself; to the last; living legend; man's unconquerable will; master of his fate; captain of his soul. What we have is a group of phrases others have used, over and over. Some, like "life, liberty, and the pursuit of happiness" and "master of my fate and captain of my soul" are quotations from the work of Thomas Jefferson and William Cowper, though both are often used by many who do not know from whom they quote or perhaps even that they quote. The rest may have no recognizable source, and perhaps not everyone reading them here has read them before, but all in fact are sufficiently known as phrases so that most people who read "during the few weeks of life" can supply "left" as the next verb almost without reading it; "unbounded" is followed by "energy" and "unquenchable" by "thirst" and we know and expect this.

This is the first and easiest way to think about cliches. They are trite or hackneyed words or phrases used by writers over and over until they have lost whatever freshness they may once have had. Looked at this way, the fault inheres in the words, so that one can underline the phrase "living legend" and say, "That is a cliche." The implication of this is that the writer should avoid cliches and can do so by not using phrases he has read in books or heard in speeches. The passage I have constructed is filled with cliches, but most of the examples given earlier in this book have their share. In the first paper quoted in Chapter 2 I find the following: "schools nowadays," "do an admirable job," "as is evidenced by," "beyond the temporary hardships," "a good education is an extremely valuable commodity," "commands a high salary," and all in the first paragraph. None of these phrases has quite the inevitable thump of "living legend," but all can easily be found, existing as phrases, in many other places besides this paper.

If a cliche is a phrase that has been used over and over and so has lost its power, the objection to cliches must be that the writer who uses them is not an original writer. This is the way the matter is usually put: cliches, trite words and phrases are dead, stale, flat, the sign of a writer who borrows rather than creates. There is much to be said for arguing the matter this way. What is wrong with almost all writing on almost all the sports pages in America is simply that almost all sports writers use the same cliches, so that almost all sports events are allowed to fall into the same patterns as those dictated by the cliches. What is wrong with most writing done in courses in composition given for freshmen in college is simply that almost all the writers use the same cliches. The advice to students is obvious: avoid these trite words, be original.

There is something wrong with this analysis of the problem, however, that I can begin to get at by saying that almost no one takes this advice. Writers who have been told that their writing is full of cliches very often avoid using those cliches for which they were first criticized, but almost inevitably they use others, and they do so because they have been asked to think of cliches as particular words and phrases. If, however, the writer tries to avoid all words so much in everyday use that they are understood by all, he will soon find there are no words left except a few that no one will understand if he uses them. On the one hand, then, we must understand that a cliche is not simply a small catalogue of overworked phrases which, if avoided, will be so felt by their absence that the style will brighten and sparkle. On the other hand, we must understand that a cliche is not just any common idiom. Either way, we must begin to look somewhere other than in the phrases themselves to see what makes a phrase a cliche.

Let's go back to the first of the examples offered above and ask if there is a better way of describing what is wrong than simply saying that all the phrases are cliches. That much is so obviously true that it may seem strange to feel the need to say more. But let us see what can be gained if we imagine the writer of these phrases to be a student who has never heard of the word "cliche," who very much approves of his own writing, and who is indignant at being called down for work he happens to admire. "What's wrong with cliches?" he asks. "They are words you have taken from somewhere else," is the quick answer. But, he says, "So are the words 'they are the words you have taken from somewhere else'; *those* words aren't yours." "But your words make you sound as though you yourself had nothing to say and as though the character you are describing here, this David, isn't something you have seen for yourself. He is only a composite of other people's phrases about people who aren't David."

This last answer may seem pretty good, and the hypothetical teacher who says this might feel the matter can rest there. Surely the student can see that he has some obligation to express what he sees, not what someone else has seen? Yes, he can see that. But, the student goes on, "If I say David was six feet tall, weighed two hundred pounds, had blonde hair and a big dimple in his chin just like Kirk Douglas', aren't I using other people's words to express what I see? And isn't this the only thing I've done that you don't like? Do you think this description I have given you is full of cliches?" No, it isn't, at least not by most definitions of a cliche. "But in the second description," answers the hypothetical teacher, "you have begun to take the words of others and express what you see. Cliches aren't just the words that are used. When you say David had a dimple in his chin like Kirk Douglas' I think you have seen something, compared it with something else you've seen, something someone else might not have seen just as you have."

Our teacher may be still a long way away from making clear to the student just what is wrong, but the moment he can show why cliches aren't just the words that are used, he has made the most important first step away from mouthing the usual cliches about what is wrong with cliches. The language is everyone's and for everyone's use, and all languages acquire idioms which everyone must use to make himself understood. For me to say our teacher is probably "still a long way," and that "he has made the first step," is to employ metaphors so deeply ingrained in our language that they have become idioms, which means that the moment I write "still a long . . . ," the reader can almost by himself supply the "way" he knows is coming next. Indeed, some idioms are so deeply worked into our language that any alteration in the words is likely to seem only a self-conscious attempt at doing something different; we say "instead *of*" and "rather *than*," "come *upon*" and "happen *on*," we "consider" a person to be an honest man, and "regard" him "*as*" an honest man. None of these is ever called a cliche, yet most descriptions of cliches cover idioms as well.

The difference lies not in the words but in the mind that uses them, and there is no phrase, no matter how common, no matter how often it has been abused in the past, that cannot be used well by someone who tries to use it well. Considered just simply as phrases, the difference between a cliche and an idiom is one of intent; people tend to use cliches to impress others, and idioms hardly ever can be made to do this. But the real question is one of alertness, not whether one borrows (that is unavoidable), but how. A cliche is the result of someone's seeking to be impressive, convincing, persuasive, when that is all he is trying to be, and his language is simply an instrument of rhetorical power and not an instrument to express thought and feeling. The language in a cliche is dead, not because it is worn and familiar or overused, but because it is used thoughtlessly, and in a context that implies or demands thoughtfulness: "True to himself to the last, he became a living legend, a symbol of man's unconquerable will to be the master of his fate and the captain of his soul." Instead of underlining phrases and calling them cliches, let us ask questions: in what sense can a man be master of his fate when he is about to die? do *all* men have an unconquerable will? is it the will of all men that they be masters of their fate? if he was being true to himself, what is the self to which he was true? how does one decide if a given action shows a man being true to himself? is a living legend the same thing as a famous man? The sentence and the paragraph do not answer these questions, and do not even acknowledge that these are real questions. The writer gestures at being impressive, but behind the gestures there is nothing impressive in thought or feeling.

A phrase or sentence can be a cliche the first time it is used; it does not have to wait until it becomes the cant of hack writers to earn that title. This happens a great deal in political oratory and propaganda, where often the effort is to produce slogans or battle cries that the listeners *will* be impressed by and *won't* ask questions about. For instance:

> We hold these truths to be self-evident, that all men are created equal, that they are endowed by their Creator with certain unalienable rights, that among these are Life, Liberty, and the pursuit of Happiness.

> And so, my fellow Americans, ask not what your country can do for you; ask what you can do for your country.

I pick these in part because they are well known, in part because both were cliches from the moment they were written, in part because they were written by justly famous and great men whose fame can stand criticism of their best-known rallying cries. As such, as words to be repeated so as to unite and even inspire, they have done their work well. But look: in what sense are men created equal? is it self-evident the ways in which they are? in what sense does the Creator, any Creator, endow his creation with rights? how can these rights be unalienable when, since the beginning of time, they have been denied to exist or have been modified, even trampled on? what does the right to live mean? simply that tyrants should not execute men, or that tyrants should protect men from deadly epidemic? liberty—whose? is a child free? a black slave free? a poor man free? the pursuit of happiness—what is that? can happiness be pursued? how? Or, looking at Kennedy's sentence: are my interests and my country's interests so opposed one to another that I must drop one to gain the other? what do I give up when I ask what I can do for my country? what kind of country is it where patriotic service precludes my asking what my country gives me in return?

These questions seem worth asking, and under different circumstances Jefferson and Kennedy almost certainly would be able to give good and interesting answers to them. But, at that moment, neither man was as interested in thinking carefully as he was in being impressive and memorable, an aim both achieved very well; they were good writers of cliches. The great test for this is simply the enthusiastic response of a public that is either uninterested at the moment or unable at any time to believe that its politicians can think. Such a public goes to the cliches like iron filings to a magnet, because the cliche will provide, all at once, the easily remembered phrasing, the impressive gesture, and the cue to stop thinking. It is one of the nearly infallible tests of a cliche. Whenever a group of my students, in writing about something they have read, flock to one or two passages to quote or discuss, then I can be fairly certain that there is something defective about the passage, something loose or oversimple in its workings. It is not that the students all have terrible taste, really; it is just that the cliche gives them an easy slogan, an alluring turn of phrase, an apparently easy way out of the difficulty that the work offers them.

It is with this in mind that I want to return to the second of my examples quoted at the beginning of this section:

> There appears to be a vast amount of confusion on this point, but I do not know many Negroes who are eager to be "accepted" by white people, still less to be loved by them; they, the blacks, simply don't wish to be beaten over the head by the whites every instant of our brief passage on this planet. White people will have quite enough to do in learning how to accept and love themselves and each other, and when they have achieved this—which will not be tomorrow and may very well be never—the Negro problem will no longer exist, for it will no longer be needed.

Compare this with the first of the two examples and, of course, it seems free of what we ordinarily think of as cliches. But it is the one place in this selection from Baldwin's book that students flock to; it is the one anyone might mark as a sentence nicely enough turned to be good ammunition against bigots. This should be a sign to the wary that something is wrong, and what is originally striking is so because it is only striking, only flashy.

As we have seen, the greatness of this piece of Baldwin's lies in its care, its eager refusal to take the experience of adolescence simply. What we have here is a momentary pause in this loving remembrance and assessment of his past, a pause that immediately lapses into cliche. Throughout the piece Baldwin makes us aware that white power shaped his world even though no whites appear as such. He also shows the way in which all blacks, regardless of who they were, lived in the same world. That is to say, Baldwin allows for certain generalizations about white and black, though I suspect it is easier to know such generalizations are possible than it is to know just what they are. But in this passage Baldwin stops what he is doing and becomes a black man addressing a white audience, and the moment he does that he becomes a propagandist, a writer concerned with making the whites feel guilty. Such a goal is a simple goal, and Baldwin is a splendid writer, so he can achieve his goal quickly and easily. When he says that "they, the blacks, simply don't wish to be beaten over the head by the whites every instant of our brief passage on this planet," the first question has to be: what has "this planet" got to do with it? and what difference does it make how brief or long "our brief passage is"? But then, who is being beaten over the head? Young Baldwin as he looks for a gimmick? The pimps and drifters on the Avenue? Then he says, "White people will have quite enough to do in learning how to accept and love themselves." Do whites have this problem more than others? Has any large group, especially when it had power, ever been able to accept and love itself? And when the white's Negro problem no longer exists, what about the Negro's Negro problem?

Baldwin has taken his eye off his subject. If we are really to learn of the fire next time, it will not be because of writing like this, but because Baldwin is able to be so beautiful and complicated about being himself and being black that inevitably the question arises: if this lovely, sensitive man wants to set fires, what can we expect from someone less lovely, less sensitive, less able to find the kind of gimmick Baldwin found in writing? My response is a white man's response, and the wonder of Baldwin's book is that though it is mostly a book written for white men, only occasionally does it become nakedly, simplistically, and tritely a book designed to increase white folks' guilt. The problem may be a problem of black and white, but for Baldwin to treat himself, as he does here, simply as a black man, is for him to treat himself with the same indifference to being James Baldwin that he finds so embittering or hateful when he encounters it in a white man. When Baldwin is only black, when he makes me only white, then cliches and slogans are bound to be written.

Metaphors: Live, Dead, and Silly

In a way, metaphor is the heart of the problem, for any writer with a decent understanding of metaphor is probably going to avoid jargon and cliches as a matter of instinctive survival, and is probably also going to begin to see ways of making his style become what he wants it to be. Up to now in this chapter I have talked about what goes wrong in a style, and a good deal of this discussion is a critique of bad and silly metaphors, but some things can be said about metaphor that might prove to be a positive help to someone struggling with his own style.

I may only be betraying my own ignorance, but the way metaphor usually is taught seems to invite my students to think of it as an ornament to their style, an effect achieved in poetry but not really necessary for any decent, hard-working plain style. As a result, most students seem unaware of the way metaphor pervades even the plainest and most hard-working of styles, and is the dominant feature of almost all our speech. Students seem to feel that metaphor is something they can "use" or not "use" as they wish, and so when they decide to use metaphors, they become wildly self-conscious and liable to cliche. When asked, they speak of metaphor as something different from a simile. "The moon was a ghostly galleon tossed upon stormy seas," they have learned, is a metaphor, and "My love is like a red, red rose" is a simile. Their examples, as I say, come from poems; metaphors are what you learn about in English classes, nowhere else.

The definition of metaphor most students have carried with them from English class to English class, however, can serve a wider purpose than it usually does. A metaphor is a comparison in which one thing is said to *be* another thing, as opposed to a simile, which is a comparison in which one thing is said to be *like* another thing. The distinction may have its purpose, but a moment's reflection will show that when one thing is said to *be* another thing, that does not mean that it in fact *is* that other thing but only that it is *like* that thing; metaphors and similes do exactly the same thing. When I say, in the first sentence of this paragraph, that students "have carried" a definition of metaphor from class to class, I do not mean that this carrying is literally the same carrying one might do if the subject were a ball of twine, but only that what students do with their definition of metaphor is *like* what they might do with a ball of twine. The word "carry" is a metaphor here, then. Look at the words "show" and "do" in the third sentence of this paragraph. These are obviously not felt as metaphors, yet they obviously are not meant to be taken literally; a moment's reflection cannot "show," a metaphor cannot "do" or be "felt" except metaphorically.

You can take almost any passage and treat it like the pictures in which you try to find the hidden animals. How many metaphors can you find in the following:

> Sure, I see Joe Fisher every morning. He comes in after class, scrounges around until he finds someone with a dime, buys his coffee and then he parks himself off in the corner. Within five minutes the son-of-a-bitch is holding court with a bunch of women. It's incredible. He sits back, pounds his spoon on the table, blows smoke down their throat, looks bored, yet somehow he manages it all so as to seem the biggest thing in their world. I've seen girls who wouldn't give me the time of day and to whom

I've been princely treat him like some guru. It's as though he digs some language or tunes in on some obscure wave length made just for Joe Fisher and women.

Without stretching the idea of metaphor very much, I count nineteen: scrounges, parks, son-of-a-bitch, holding court, bunch, incredible, pounds, blows smoke down their throat, manages, biggest thing, world, seen, give me the time of day, princely, guru, digs some language, tunes in on some wave length, obscure, made. And that doesn't count those that are like metaphors, even if one doesn't want to call them that: every morning, someone with a dime, within five minutes, all, treat. Within a hundred words Joe Fisher is a rodent, a car, a male offspring of a female dog, a king, a stage director, a wise man, a mystic, a favored child of nature for whom things are "made."

Granted that an unprepared speech in conversation has the highest metaphorical density of any language we use, the game can be played even in conversations where everything is short bursts, with newspapers, with dialogue in movies. Our sense of the world involves us so constantly and completely in metaphors that there is little exaggeration in saying that all our speech and writing approaches metaphor; for example, you can hear many people who don't know what a metaphor is make one out of "literally" when they say, "He literally brought the house down," by which, of course, it is not to be understood that that is what he literally did.

Given the way metaphors pervade our speech, a few statements are perhaps in order. A metaphor is a kind of lie or untruth: something is said to be something that it is not. "He parks himself in the corner" compares Joe to an automobile. Unpacking the metaphor, we can say, "Joe is like an automobile in the way he finds his place of rest," or, simply, "Joe is an automobile," or, "Joe is an automobile in this respect." We cannot, nor do we want to, say, "An automobile is Joe." If a metaphor were not a metaphor, it would be an identity and therefore reversible, as in "Sunrise is the beginning of day" and "The beginning of day is sunrise." There is a kind of magic in our key verb "to be," such that it cannot only make equalities and definitions but can also state or imply likenesses between two things that aren't each other and do not, in most respects, resemble each other, like Joe and an automobile. Likewise, metaphors are not capable of replacing each other; "Joe parks himself in the corner" is okay, and so is "The car parks hard," but "Joe parks hard" won't do. All this is perhaps elementary enough, but it can have consequences that are not always easy to determine, so it is best to get the elementary things straight. One of the basic tasks of intelligent living is to understand the extent to which certain statements which use some form of "to be" are statements of identity: "God is . . . ," "My country is . . . ," "You are . . ." Most really important statements about the human condition or the nature of the universe are of the form "x is y," and if "You are the promised kiss of springtime" is only a rather pretty and confused pile-up of metaphors, what are we to say of "God is the Father Almighty"? In any event, we must see that though many metaphors do not take the grammatical form of "x is y," all metaphors can be transformed into statements of that pattern and often can best be understood and evaluated when this transformation is made. This is especially true when the metaphor lies in a verb—"Joe scrounged," "Joe parked," "Joe held court"—and the fact that the statement is metaphorical is apt to pass unnoticed. It is often possible to examine the implications of one's own statements by taking all the metaphors and turning them into the "x is y" form, and quite often writers gain a much better grip on their writing when they practice doing this. If nothing else, to take a paragraph of one's own writing and to unpack and rephrase all its metaphors is to see what a strange and wonderful instrument the language is and how much control it is possible to exert over one's use of it.

Here, for instance, is a paragraph with some rather interesting metaphors that its author probably was unaware he was using:

> In Sherwood Anderson's "I Want to Know Why," only one of the characters is described in depth. Here we see a boy whose entire life has but one goal, to be a trainer or a jockey. His dreams are the dreams of a young boy, not those of a grown man. Hopping freights, exploring strange places, living only for his moments at the stables and the track—these are described so

vividly the reader can feel them. The boy's life centers around the track, and as long as this is so, the boy's world is secure. The races are always there, along with the parade of new colts. The boy depends heavily on the horses for this way of life.

Let's again list the metaphors: in depth, see, entire life, dreams, grown man, hopping freights, exploring strange places, moments, feel, centers around, world, secure, always there, parade, depends heavily, way of life. What I want to look at especially are those which are so much a part of the way we speak that the metaphorical quality of the phrase is not easy to see. First, though, a word about "centered around," which must be the commonest mixed metaphor in the present use of the language. A mixed metaphor is not simply two consecutive metaphors; "That man is a snake, a rat" is simply a change of metaphor. A mixed metaphor is an absurdity that arises when someone is not aware that he is using a metaphor: "We pulverized them into sending up the white flag" is such a mix, because to pulverize something is to leave it in no condition to send up white flags; "The foundation of his position must flounder" is mixed because, of the many wonderful things metaphorical foundations can do, floundering is not one. The term "centered around" is, in this sense, self-contradictory, because to center on something is to be, metaphorically, at the one point incapable of motion—around, through, by, or any other way. What happens, of course, is that people forget that "to center" is a metaphor in itself and so demands a preposition appropriate to the action of centering.

Mixed metaphors, however, are really an interesting sidelight, and most writers learn early to avoid them. More important are the metaphors in this paragraph that silently construct this writer's "world": in depth, world, secure. The questions raised by metaphors of depth and shallowness really ask us who we think we are and how we see others. The writer here says that only the boy in this story "is described in depth." One way of stating the curiosity of the problem is to point out that almost certainly this writer means that the boy is the only character described "at length." Surely, "in depth" and "at length" should not mean the same thing, but the fact that they do tells us

[157]

something. Most studies that are carried on in depth are carried on longer than other studies, but whatever else is implied by "in depth" is seldom made clear. Presumably, to be deep is not to be shallow, and a study in depth would explore the deeps, the profundities, the complexities, of a person or a problem. Presumably, also, one could carry on at great length, that is, for a long time, about a problem and never explore its depths. The difficulty is that no one will ever confess this, because if an analysis that takes five minutes is not deep, no one expected it could be, but an analysis that takes far longer ought to be far deeper. So it is that we presume, or let others presume for us, that length makes depth. It is possible, though in our world it is not allowed to be possible, that someone can be deep about someone else in a single sentence, and it is not only possible but likely that most people can go on at length about a problem without ever being deep. As long as length and depth are allowed to measure the same things, however, no one is apt to find this out, and the confusion of metaphorical reality can only be a really long and deep confusion.

Now, "world," that most fashionable of metaphors. "The boy's world is secure," says the passage; professional football or fashion or Henry Orient or youth or marijuana or almost everything else one can name is said to have its own "world," or "sphere" (it used to be only a "niche"). In James Baldwin's world, in the world of Harlem, in the modern world, in my world, and each time the metaphor is used the implication grows stronger that each item that has a world is isolated from everything else in creation. "This is my Father's world," says the hymn, but that is not the way the term is used now; the metaphor says that it is not all of us, or the physical body known as the earth, but some small segment thereof, that is its world. If someone tells me that I do not live in his world, he implies that the gap between my world and his is so great that I cannot possibly know what his life is like. It is as though there were no common inheritance of humanity, of a Western tradition, of American life, that is shared; each lives in his own world, each peers out onto a universe of strangers, each finds his own world made up of himself and a few other like-minded people. I have, throughout this book, spoken as though the classroom were a separate world, and have constantly deplored the fact that the metaphor may speak truly. It is a common metaphor, and if what it implies is true, then it is hard to know how we are going to get along in "the world."

Finally, "secure" and "security." My dictionary does not really think that the word as it is used in this sentence is metaphorical any longer: "The boy's world is secure," and "secure" here means "free from or not exposed to danger." What is interesting here is the way in which the term so often is used in a context that implies transience, fragility, and danger. The writer here says: "The boy's life centers around the track, and as long as this is so, the boy's world is secure." We know, thus, that the security is temporary. It is a word most often used by or about people who do not feel in the least safe; or, it may be said, people who live in their own "world" tend to use the word "secure" but seldom feel as the word or metaphor implies they do. Here are some common usages:

I don't ever feel very secure when called upon to speak. [Here "secure" means comfortable or relaxed.]

She needs more security than he will ever be able to give her. [Here "security" means steadiness.]

If he gets the best job, he will feel secure. [Here "security" almost means valuable.]

The moment he gets outside the security of the classroom, he fumbles and feels lost. [Here "security" means protection.]

What we have here is a spectrum of meanings for "secure," no one clearly literal or metaphorical, no one quite like any of the others, so that the word has a solidity of tone but no solidity of meaning. Such a word is harder to use than "in depth" or "world" when what one needs is a sense that the word *is* a metaphor. The word "security," like the word "real," can be used well only by someone who is fully aware of its different shadings and nuances. It is a word that has come to prominence precisely because what it describes or implies is so seldom felt, and the word often seems like a cry for help from someone who knows there is no help. "If he gets that job, he will feel secure"

[*159*]

is a harmless enough sentence, but the "he" it describes is no fun to contemplate at all, for any "he" that needs this or that job to feel secure is quite obviously never going to feel secure, no matter what job he gets. "She needs more security than he will ever be able to give her" means "She must marry a rock, nothing else will save her." "I don't ever feel secure when called upon to speak" means, really, "I don't ever feel secure." As a result, though "secure" and "security" themselves are not, in the strict sense, metaphors as used most of the time, they can be used as a means of avoiding a gnawing sense of pathos, loneliness, and insecurity when their potential meanings are clear to both user and reader or listener.

I have concentrated on the three words discussed above because they were the ones the paragraph offered, and I have done so only to show the kind of awareness about metaphor that any concentrated thought about writing can provoke. Three other words would call for a quite different discussion but not for a different awareness. Metaphor is how we live because it is the way we relate what we see to what we know: this is like that. The only sentences we can construct that are really without metaphors are those we construct just to prove we can do it. Care in the use of metaphor is tantamount to careful writing; sloppiness in the use of metaphor is the same thing as sloppy writing. The best and only way I know to become aware of this is to perform exercises like those I've been doing in the last few pages. Take something you have written that you are rather proud of, or maybe just something that seems all right but from which you don't see how to go on. List its metaphors, unpack a few of the obvious ones, then a few of the hidden ones that may or may not seem like metaphors to you. All of a sudden, instead of being a great writer or a drudge, you are aware of yourself for what, most importantly, you are—a user of words.

I would like to close this section on a somewhat lighter note, by considering a few of the lovely usages that come to us from advertising. Ads themselves will be with us always, but the particular ads come and go so fast that I have no hope that those I mention will still be in use a year or two from now. Certain phrases keep coming up, though, and the new ads of the future will probably only be variations on them. One class of phrases has to do with the inflated noun: "science knows," "doctors say," "tests prove," "experiments show." An ordinary third-grader knows there is something phony about these phrases, but the fun is in ferreting out what it is. The word "science" in the phrase "science knows" is a metaphor, obviously, but for what? Let us say that "Science knows acid indigestion is caused by gas bubbles," just to take a homely example. Who knows this? Science? Obviously, science is not a knower at all, nor, as it is sometimes called upon to be, a speaker ("science says"). "Scientists" is an improvement, but not much of one—what scientists? How do they know it? Most scientists are busy doing whatever it is they do and know nothing about acid indigestion beyond what they hear in advertisements. Presumably, there exists a group of doctors or medical specialists who are "good on" digestion and indigestion, but the difficulty with asking them is that they either will all agree on the assertion that "acid indigestion is caused by gas bubbles" because (I suspect) it is obvious, or else they will quarrel quite violently with the admen and among themselves over the precise definitions of "indigestion," "gas," and "bubbles." Which leads us to this: the word "science" in the assertion "Science knows acid indigestion is caused by gas bubbles" means "people who watch this ad."

One more example. "The coating on this razor blade reduces the pull to a fraction." To what fraction of what? The phrase implies that the pull is reduced so much that you can barely feel it. But what if the pull were reduced to nine-tenths (a fraction) of the pull felt when a sharp stone is scraped along the cheek? The terms of the phrase given in the ad would be fulfilled, but something would happen to our sense of how miraculous the blade is, how much in need we are of a tour of the blade's edge given by a man in a white coat.

Some "Rules" and Words About Grammar

By this point in the book, I do not need to stress that writing is not a matter of obeying rules, grammatical or otherwise. And I have said or implied at a number of places along the way my belief that most of what we know about grammar we knew before we were ever asked to write a sentence. It is one of the great mysteries that between the ages of eighteen months and three years children develop from a spoken language of a few words to a spoken language of many sentences. After age four or five, what remains for most people to learn about grammar is not grammar at all, but precision in the use of particular words. Unfortunately, when grammar is taught in schools, it is usually taught as a matter of labels and rules, so that most students' instinctive grasp of grammatical relationships is made stiff, self-conscious, and often less secure and correct than it was before.

Some things about grammar and syntax can be explained and some cannot, and perhaps the one real "rule" about these matters is that if something cannot be explained it is not really very important. I cannot say why the following is incorrect: "He felt like Casey did just after 'mighty Casey had struck out.'" The rule about "like" and "as" says that you use "like" when what lies on the other side of the conjunction has no verb, so that the following are all correct: "He felt like Casey," "He felt like Casey at the bat," or even "He felt like Casey when he struck out," where the verb "struck" is not part of the same clause as the "like." If a verb is to follow in the same clause, then you use "as": "He felt as Casey did when . . ."; "Winstons taste good as cigarettes should." That is the rule, but I cannot do more than enunciate it. Why it exists I do not know and have never heard a good explanation. I think people who are at all interested in speaking and writing correctly should learn how to use "like" and "as," and I always circle misuses of these words on students' papers, just as I circle misspelled words. But I do not think it is a very important matter, and certainly do not think that good writing or a good sense of grammar depends on such things.

The trouble comes when students think that all grammatical problems are like this one, capable of being made into a rule known to teachers but incapable of being explained. I also circle dangling modifiers and write "dangling modifier" in the margin, knowing as I do that many students who see that phrase think it is no different from my "like/as" somewhere else in the margin, and if they never ask or I never tell them, they probably will continue to treat all grammar as a matter of unexplainable rules. Here are two dangling modifiers:

> Sitting on the front porch, the chestnut tree looked huge.
> After William died, he felt there was nothing left to live for.

The modifier in each case is the phrase before the comma. Because neither is complete in itself, it attaches itself to the first noun after the comma, and in these instances produce nonsense: it is not the chestnut tree but someone looking at it that is sitting on the front porch; after William died "he" cannot still be feeling. These particular cases are corrected very simply: "As the boy sat on the front porch, the chestnut tree seemed huge to him," or "Sitting on the front porch, the boy thought the chestnut tree looked huge"; "After William died, George felt there was nothing left to live for," or "George felt there was nothing left to live for after William died." When a phrase or clause not in itself complete begins a sentence, it must attach itself to the first noun in the subsequent or main clause, so all you need to do is to see what attaches itself to what: "After carefully studying the report, economics seemed to him indeed the dismal science" is nonsense because "studying" in the opening clause should attach itself to "him" rather than "economics." The moment you get used to asking what goes with what, spotting danglers is easy, even when they are not neatly set up at the beginning of the sentence: "When he saw the girl, he saw there would be trouble walking down the gangplank." Here the phrase "walking down the gangplank" presumably should be attached to "he" and not to "trouble"; as written, the sentence can make sense only if the sight of the girl so intoxicated the man that he then would have trouble walking down the gangplank.

The only rule involved in considering dangling modifiers is the one we all know—perhaps without knowing we know it—which says that verbs modify the nearest available noun. The writer who dangles a modifier simply has not seen what he has in fact written. Of course, if his experience with teachers in the past has terribly intimidated him, he may simply cringe at the sight of any phrase which describes a grammatical point, and then never ask why his sentence had been circled or rewritten. But if he simply asks what sense is made by what he has written, he will probably have no trouble, for grammar is designed to make language intelligible. Take the familiar fact that "everyone" is a singular noun and so should have singular pronouns and verbs attached to it: "Everyone makes his own rules," not "Everyone makes their own rules." The problem here is not ignorance of the fact that singular nouns take singular pronouns and verbs—everyone learns that when learning to speak. The problem is seeing why "everyone" is a singular noun when other apparently similar nouns like "the people" or "the rest" are plural: "The people make their own decisions"; "The rest find their way home." So we need to ask what "everyone" means, and that is easily done by dividing it into the two words it combines: "every" and "one." We know that "one" is a singular noun, and "everyone" merely refers to many different "one's" without making them into a group that can act as a group. "Everyone is going to feel the pinch" means each one is going to feel the pinch, separately and in his own way, not collectively. "The people know best" means something quite different from "Everyone knows best." The people are a group, acting as a group, while everyone is many different persons, each acting individually. What we need to make these distinctions is not knowledge of grammar but simple confidence in the intelligibility of the language and in our ability to make it so.

At this point I could begin to consider some grammatical problems which are far more complicated than those I have been discussing. Many questions about the language could be asked which make my rather rough-and-ready contentions, that the language is really intelligible and that we all have most of the grammar we need, seem much less tenable. But I see little point in asking students to become consciously engaged in such questions and the problems they raise until long after they have seen how fascinating relationships among words can be. They will not, there is much evidence to show, become fascinated by "learning grammar." It seems to me that a much more normal and sensible way to become aware of English grammar is to learn a foreign language, especially one like German or Latin, which employs a grammar quite different from that of English.

What the foreign language does is simply to make one aware that those grammatical relationships which we have long since become used to in English are not laws or rules but simply our way of stating things. English, for instance, has only two genuine tenses, a present and a past, and all other statements of time or mood are made with auxiliaries: "will go," "could go," "could have gone," and so forth. I have never known what this fact implies about us, though I think it is something quite important, and I also have felt that one reason for my not knowing is that I have never become truly at home in a language that has more tenses. Just learning about the past and the imperfect tenses in French and Spanish showed me a great deal about possible ways of stating things that are less important to us, apparently, than they are to people who speak romance languages. If we have no established way to state habitual or continuous actions, such as are expressed in an imperfect tense, we must, therefore, feel differently from a Frenchman or a Spaniard about such actions.

But for the average writer, such speculations probably cannot be very fruitful. What he needs is a sense that the language he currently uses is a strange and rich instrument, capable of expressing what he wants to express. There is no reason to believe that the specialized study of grammar and language necessarily makes him a better writer, whereas it is certain that if he believes the grammar he uses is in fact intelligible to him, that can do wonders for his ability to be precise. I know no way to generate such a belief; the most I can offer is my sense that any inquiry into grammar that seeks to find out if the language makes sense ends up making the language sensible.

I want to end this section and chapter by talking about one apparently small but interesting and even important matter of tenses that arises whenever the task involved is writing about literature or another art form. Both the following sentences are grammatically correct: "William Faulkner *wrote The Sound and the Fury*," and "William Faulkner *writes* in a number of styles in *The Sound and the Fury*." Faulkner lived and died like any other man, and much can be said about him only in the past tense, generally whatever has to do with Faulkner considered as a man. But Faulkner was also a writer, and what he wrote was not and is not subject to the same process of living and dying

[165]

undergone by Faulkner the man. We do not say *The Sound and the Fury* "was," because it was, is, and will be, and like every other book it "is" every time someone starts reading it. So, too, the Faulkner that is "in" the novel "is" whenever anyone reads his words. When I write "Faulkner said . . . ," I am referring to the man who, at some moment in the past, said something; when I write "Faulkner says . . . ," I am referring to the author whose words "are" because I "am" reading them. Faulkner said what he said, but he also keeps on speaking.

Likewise, if I say, "The violins *came* in too soon during the overture," I am referring to a particular playing by some particular violinists at a particular moment in the past; if I say, "The violins *come* in after the trumpets," I am referring to a sequence of events in a piece of music, a sequence that can exist without any actual violins or trumpets ever having, in fact, played the notes that make the sequence. The music, like Faulkner's novel, or a painting of Van Gogh's, is capable of being repeated an infinite number of times; all it takes is for someone to hear it or read it or see it. Man, houses, cultures, all are caught in a temporal process that is denied by a work of art.

So, too, with characters in a story. Shakespeare's Hamlet is no more alive now than he ever was, because his existence is not subject to the laws which governed Shakespeare and govern us. In a sense, Hamlet lived and died, but in another sense he never lived and so cannot die. Quite often students will write about Hamlet or some other character entirely in the past tense: "Hamlet knew Claudius killed his father, so he planned to take his revenge. He also knew no one else knew about the murder, so he had to be careful how he behaved with Gertrude, Ophelia, Polonius, and the rest." The writer here has forgotten that Hamlet is not a person—and the mistake can be fatal. If, for instance, Hamlet were a person, he would have a grandfather, need sleep and food, find out about the weather, and sometimes be taken sick. But Hamlet is not a person, and what is true about him is only what Shakespeare wrote in the play, and there Hamlet has no grandfather, needs neither food nor sleep, never speaks of the weather, and his physical health is never in question. When we read and write about him, it is essential to remember all this, for when we do not we can get into trouble. Of any person (and *some* characters) we can ask, for instance, if they are sexual virgins, and we can expect an answer. We can also ask if Hamlet is a virgin, but there is no answer, and we cannot say that because Hamlet "is a man" that he must, like living and dying men, be or not be a virgin. Shakespeare offers no evidence; therefore, there can be no answer. If we insist on speculating about Hamlet's sexual experience, we will probably begin to slip into the past tense, and we will certainly begin ignoring the Hamlet of Shakespeare's play and begin inventing our own private Hamlets. This may seem a simple enough truth, but the illusion that characters are people is one that dies very hard.

Hamlet has a mother and had a father, but no grandfather. Goldilocks, on the other hand, has neither parents nor grand-parents—and gets along well enough without them. Once one gets in the habit of getting the tenses right, such facts need not seem strange.

5

CONCLUSION

In Chapter 3, when speaking about conclusions, I argued that they can serve no useful purpose if they are only mirror images for introductions or summaries of the plot. The general outlines of my argument in this book have been repeated often enough up to now, anyway. What I would like to do here is to address myself briefly to an issue raised by one reader of the book in manuscript. He said he liked some of my analyses of particular compositions very much, but wanted to know if such lengthy discussions were intended to serve as models for the way I thought all student papers should be analyzed, corrected, and graded. If, in short, I aimed to do anything more than offer comfort and advice to some beleaguered "good students" and "bad students," what did I have in mind? Did I mean to be leader in some revolution in courses in composition? These questions were addressed one teacher to another, but I see no reason why students should not be apprised of what I take to be the facts in our present circumstances.

To say that institutions and systems have had a deadening effect on the way writing is taught and learned in schools is to be a reporter, not a revolutionary; to try to do something about it in one's own classrooms simply makes one a teacher. Were I a revolutionary, I suppose I would have to have, at the very least, a counterproposal, an alternative institution, method, or system—and I have no desire to try to offer any of these. I do believe, however, that teachers, departments, or school systems have an obligation to themselves and to their students to say what they think they are doing and why, and I don't think anywhere near enough are fulfilling this obligation. Somewhere along the line a simple sense of purpose has been lost, jettisoned, abandoned to committees, and most courses in composition in high school and college are simply the meeting ground for a number of different groups, all with different axes to grind, none really much interested in teaching or learning writing—not opposed to writing, but not interested in it either.

We can begin with the outsiders. Administrators, trustees, and legislators tend to look upon courses in composition with a mixture of horror, nostalgia, and scepticism. They are horrified because teaching English is, relatively speaking, an expensive proposition. Teachers of English do not demand great laboratories or lavish field trips, and they do not command huge salaries, but there are so many of them. In many colleges and most universities, the course in Freshman English is required and the teacher is insistent that there be no more than twenty-five students in a class, and so there are more sections of that course and more English teachers than in any other course and department. Outsiders are also nostalgic, because they tend to remember, or to invent, a time in the past when people "really learned how to write," when "students who couldn't spell or write complete sentences were failed, and that was that." If they ask a teacher of English what goes on in his writing courses, they then become sceptical that it is worth the time and effort being put into it. There aren't as many teachers flatly insistent on correct spelling, precise punctuation, or neat copies as there used to be. So the question of administrators, trustees, and legislators is: how can we expect students to learn to write competently when English teachers won't insist on competent performances?

Generally speaking, faculty members in other departments feel the same way. Most people who have received some degree beyond a high-school diploma feel they themselves write decently enough, and many tend to deplore the way others write. In proportion to their estimate of their own writing, they will find in courses in writing a target for their complaint that writing is not being decently taught any more.

[170]

Next we should consider English teachers. Most of them never had a good course in composition, and so they are dubious whether there can be such a course. By and large, teaching composition is for them the most onerous part of their duties. Teachers in high schools and junior colleges often feel in an inferior position to teachers in colleges, and that sense of inferiority is easily measured by the number of hours they spend teaching in writing courses when compared with their colleagues in four-year colleges, who spend relatively little time in such courses. Most English teachers are English teachers in the first place because they are interested in literature, and most of the time teaching writing is distinct in their minds from teaching literature, and they would much rather do the latter. As a result they do what they can to extricate themselves from assignments in writing courses and to transform courses ostensibly in writing into courses in literature. Because they usually hold the whip hand when it comes to deciding what goes into writing courses, the teachers of literature tend to fill these courses with poems, plays, and novels, and to spend little time talking with students about writing. This is true at almost all levels, from junior high on up, and in colleges the trend is away from having or requiring a course in composition for freshmen. Indeed, were it not that such courses provide a good way to give employment and teaching experience to graduate students, more schools would abandon the enterprise altogether than have already. Those schools which keep the requirement tend to give the course as a survey of English or American literature or as a means of focusing on something meant "to excite the students," like existentialism or violence in modern America. Anything but a course that emphasizes writing.

Finally, we must consider the students. Most of them, like most of their English or Language Arts teachers, cannot imagine there is such a thing as a good course in writing. To work on writing, for most, has been a matter of drill and learning rules, and they want no more of it than they need to keep climbing the scholastic ladder. By the time most students arrive in college, if they have any pleasant memories at all of an English teacher, it is invariably a teacher who didn't teach writing but who had heated discussions of current issues or moral problems in his class. They are required to take Freshman English for a term or a year, and if their teacher cannot explain why he wants to participate in a course in writing, they will probably do as little as possible in that course, and, as I have said before, the good student can do very little indeed and still come out quite well.

So the outsiders tend to want courses that "really teach students how to write," by which they mean teach students how to be competent. So the insiders tend to want as little of that as possible and to welcome any modification in the direction of working with literature, or what is called ideas. Yet—and here is perhaps the saddest part of the whole matter—in whatever course is created out of these various pressures and desires, an enormous number of hours is spent by students and teachers in writing and reading the writing of others. No one seems to want it, or to know what to do about it, but it is the case. Students who work hard and students who turn out competent junk in an hour, teachers who labor long and teachers who seek only short cuts, all seem to hate the present situation, all spend lots of time writing and reading papers. And if this is the case, and if the only solution envisaged by most people is escape by abolishing courses in writing, then what I have to say next will be of interest only to those few who are willing to take courses in writing and to make them better. I think it can be done.

Whatever the course, it has to be a real course and not just a committee's compromises. By this I mean that a course in composition should have the same kind of intellectual coherence that a course in modern American literature or medieval history should have. The reports I have received from high-school students of my acquaintance lead me to think that most of their Language Arts courses are a vaguely strung together series of units, and this is certainly true of most freshman English courses I know anything about. To be sure, such courses are organized, in the sense that they can be outlined and made to look like a coherent sequence, but they are not organized at all in the sense I spoke of earlier: class-by-class, week-by-week, a clearly felt sense of direction, of having been somewhere, of going somewhere. Furthermore, in any writing course, what offers this sense of direction should have something to do with writing— and that will seem like a truism only until you look at what goes on in nine out of ten writing courses. A course that uses for its texts an American novel and an anthology of American stories, for instance, is one that is constantly shifting its focus: Malamud here, Updike there, Henry James, Hawthorne, Peter Taylor, and Robert Penn Warren down the way. I think I can string together an argument about "the short story" and/or "America" as well as the next man, but for the most part, this argument will consist of throat-clearing transitions between stories and authors, and the students will come to recognize it as something that seems to happen maybe every Monday before anyone is fully awake. After the throat is cleared, we turn to the particular story for a class or two and act as though no other story had ever been written—and this will be true no matter how often I tell students to make comparisons between stories. Class-by-class, there is no genuine sense of direction, and especially no sense that the papers due each Friday have anything to do with each other. I grade the papers over the weekend, perhaps we talk about them for awhile or even before the whole class on Monday, then I refurbish my little argument about "the short story" or "America," and we're on to something else. Most of the time the students don't object, but I know that is because they don't believe anything different is possible. English courses have been like that for as long as they can remember, and the only changes made in recent years have been in the direction of increasing the number of things read—two novels rather than one, twenty stories rather than a dozen, a play or some poems thrown in for contrast or some such—which can only have the effect of making the act of taking such a course more and more like shopping in a supermarket.

The easiest way to correct the situation is to cut down drastically on the number of items to be considered. A dozen short stories and a novel is not too much reading for a course, but it is much too much for a course in need of coherence and in need of many classes spent discussing writing. The ideal, in any course that is going to have reading in it, is to have one book, and that book must not be an anthology. If one seeks to make the closest possible connections between what the students are reading and the problems that will be raised by their writing, a book that does not come under the usual heading of "literature" is probably best. Literature inevitably raises special problems that are, for most students, pretty remote from their sense of themselves as writers. They can write on Faulkner or Melville if told to do so, but almost certainly they are not going to feel, as they do so, that what they do as they write is at all what these writers did as they wrote. Likewise, anything written much more than a century ago affords an invitation to remoteness of a different but equally crippling kind. Fortunately, the world is filled with very good books that could provide a first-rate basis for most of a course that runs from ten to eighteen weeks. *Walden* is a book with which one can easily spend a whole class talking about a couple of paragraphs—and nothing reveals the potential density of writing better than a good class spent on a few hundred words and a book which can go on yielding its riches class after class. *The Education of Henry Adams* is almost impossible to cover in a couple of weeks, even with advanced students, because it presents a good deal that is unfamiliar to most; but in the course of a term, any student can find out what he needs to know, and to see, simultaneously, how to understand Adams' strange and wonderful tones and sense of education. I can imagine a very exciting course being made out of Newman's *The Idea of a University* and Ruskin's *Unto This Last*, another out of Mill's *On Liberty* and Arnold's *Culture and Anarchy*. Or, if all this seems much too remote from the present, George Orwell's *Homage to Catalonia* or *The Road to Wigan Pier*, Loren Eisley's *The Immense Journey* alongside Konrad Lorenz' *King Solomon's Ring*, Sybille Bedford's *The Faces of Justice* with Jane Jacobs' *Death and Life of Great American Cities*. If these still seem too remote, *The Fire Next Time*, *Armies of the Night*, and *The Autobiography of Malcolm X* are splendid books which no one can claim are terribly out-of-date. With all these books, many problems which might present themselves if they were jammed into some other course—problems caused by intricacy of argument, apparent remoteness of subject, serious flaws in tone or attitude—all can be more easily solved when there is time to relax, to fill in background, to criticize as well as to praise, to praise as well as to comprehend. It doesn't make a great deal of difference what the book is, as long as the teacher feels comfortable with it and can see ways of building sequences of classes and assignments with it. It is for this reason, by the way, that having a committee decide on what book to use almost always fails. In a fairly large department, there simply isn't one book that everyone is going to want to teach. Much better to have some of the more experienced teachers announce what book they are going to use and ask the others to choose from among the books announced, so that the resultant committees are made up of people all of whom have agreed beforehand that they want a given work to serve as their focus. Having done this, they can then decide among themselves if they want common assignments and common emphases.

Another way of constructing a course is to get rid of reading altogether. This idea usually strikes people with horror when they first hear of it—"What's the matter, don't you like students to read?"—and perhaps if I had not taught in such a course myself I would have the same response. In that course, designed and directed by Theodore Baird at Amherst, the sequence of assignments calls for one short paper for every class. The text is simply the papers themselves, handed in one day and handed back and discussed the next, thirty or so papers in the course of a semester. The great advantage of the course is that it keeps the emphasis so strongly on the papers that no student can fail to become more aware of himself as a writer, often by seeing how very well students can write without ever being self-conscious about style or learning. The great disadvantage of the course is that it requires an enormous amount of time and commitment from both teacher and student, more than most are seriously willing to give. When you have that many papers, however, students do not feel under the gun all the time, and so tend to be more willing to experiment, to try something out, to be willing to make mistakes, than they are apt to be when they have only half a dozen assignments during the course of the term.

Whatever the format of the course, it needs many ways of focusing attention on the papers students write. It may well be that no teacher could or would try to write comments on every student's paper that are as lavish as those I, in effect, have tried to write in this book on the various papers quoted. But it is not at all beyond the dreams of any teacher to spend a class trying to

CONCLUSION

do this kind of thing. Doing this is much the best way for a teacher to provide a context in which the students themselves can see how an argument is flimsy or repetitious, how another is perceptive and beautifully worked out. After much work of this kind in class, the countless squiggles that teachers put on papers, squiggles which have seemed damning and imposed at a great distance from the student, can come to seem very much like the comments a student makes in class, as he searches out explanations for why he finds something good or bad or hazy or neat. If this happens, then the course is a success, because the students can see it as a collective enterprise, and ultimately that is the real justification for any course: that the group, by working as a group, makes one or all the people in it feel more completely aware of, and in potential control of, their minds.

I know full well that if such a course were proposed to most teachers and students of English, the objection would be that the course lacked one thing. Some would call it "reading," others "culture," still others "variety" or "options," but all would mean roughly the same thing. As far as I can see, the objection is based on despair: despair of ever achieving intellectual discipline and a sense of consecutiveness, despair of seeing education and the culture as anything more than training people to move around in a supermarket of books and ideas arranged according to the Library of Congress classification system. I do not think such training is necessarily contemptible, and I certainly do not think that no one ever becomes truly educated if he goes through courses organized in an outlined, semiorganized way. I do think, however, that what is now called the "generation gap" has always existed, and that the role of the good teacher in any society is to do what he can to bridge that gap by making himself be as disciplined and as consecutive as he can be. The culture can exist as a living tradition when students can see themselves as its heirs, and they can do that best, not by haphazard reading and discussing, not by being "exposed" to the largest possible variety of cultural material, but by seeing how difficult and exciting it is to put two things together in a careful rather than in a slovenly way. One event—the meeting in a classroom of student and author—is enough. To bring these two minds into

[176]

ON WRITING

genuine relation is task enough for any teacher or student.

There I would like to let the matter rest. If we are going to offer courses in writing, if we are going to admit that the writing we seek cannot be taught, we must have courses that feel no obligation to cover a certain amount of material, that offer time for everyone to hear each other's voice, that allow the teacher to insist that much—indeed everything—is possible, and at the same time to insist he does not know what that everything is, exactly, or how to get it. Such courses must be able to accommodate generously many kinds of human waywardness: students who like to talk all the time, students who never talk, students who don't come to class more than once a week, classes that discover a whole hour has been spent on what turned out to be only an interesting digression, teachers who can't finish sentences clearly, teachers who cannot suffer foolishness as gladly as they know they should, a subject like writing that is not a subject at all but an action, a world that sometimes looks as though it has no use for disinterested conversation and common sense. All the problems that arise from being writers and being in courses where writing is the subject are like these, and because they are human problems, they cannot be solved. But they can be faced and understood and given a sense of direction that comes from believing the mind can make orders and sequences where none existed before.

Your mind is not my mind, we are not telepathic, so we must speak, and write. All the rest—the classrooms, the assignments, the subjects—are only our clumsy ways of acknowledging, and celebrating, these facts.